Defining Moments

Other books by Peter Shaw

Mirroring Jesus as Leader, Cambridge: Grove, 2004

Conversation Matters: How to Engage Effectively with One Another, London: Continuum, 2005

The Four Vs of Leadership: Vision, Values, Value-added and Vitality, Chichester, UK: Capstone, 2006

Finding Your Future: The Second Time Around, London: Darton, Longman and Todd, 2006

Business Coaching: Achieving Practical Results through Effective Engagement, Chichester, UK: Capstone, 2007 (co-authored with Robin Linnecar)

Making Difficult Decisions: How to Be Decisive and Get the Business Done, Chichester, UK: Capstone, 2008

Riding the Rapids: How to Navigate through Turbulent Times, London: Praesta, 2008 (co-authored with Jane Stephens)

Deciding Well: A Christian Perspective on Making Decisions as a Leader, Vancouver: Regent College Publishing, 2009

Raise Your Game: How to Succeed at Work, Chichester, UK: Capstone, 2009

Effective Christian Leaders in the Global Workplace, Colorado Springs: Authentic, 2010

Seizing the Future, London: Praesta, 2010 (co-authored with Robin Hindle Fisher)

DEFINING MOMENTS

Navigating through Business and Organizational Life

Peter Shaw

palgrave
macmillan

First published 2010 by
PALGRAVE MACMILLAN

Palgrave Macmillan in the UK is an imprint of Macmillan Publishers Limited,
registered in England, company number 785998, of Houndmills, Basingstoke,
Hampshire RG21 6XS.

Palgrave Macmillan in the US is a division of St Martin's Press LLC,
175 Fifth Avenue, New York, NY 10010.

Palgrave Macmillan is the global academic imprint of the above companies
and has companies and representatives throughout the world.

Palgrave® and Macmillan® are registered trademarks in the United States,
the United Kingdom, Europe and other countries.

ISBN: 978–0–230–57720–6

This book is printed on paper suitable for recycling and made from fully
managed and sustained forest sources. Logging, pulping and manufacturing
processes are expected to conform to the environmental regulations of the
country of origin.

A catalogue record for this book is available from the British Library.

A catalog record for this book is available from the Library of Congress.

10 9 8 7 6 5 4 3 2 1
19 18 17 16 15 14 13 12 11 10

Printed and bound in Great Britain by
CPI Antony Rowe, Chippenham and Eastbourne

Dedicated to Frances, with whom I have shared
many defining moments for approaching 40 years,
with thanks for her wisdom, calmness and kindness

Contents

Foreword

It was October 2008 and I was about to address the National Conference for senior leaders of Jobcentre Plus. There had been much speculation about the UK economy and, although unconfirmed at that time, the recession had just begun. I knew how capable the organization and the people who worked in it were. And I knew how big a challenge the recession posed for our organization, which had been through three years of transformation and efficiency improvements. As Chief Executive, I was responsible for enabling all the delegates to leave the conference feeling confident, with a spring in their step, ready to lead their people through demanding times. The message of my speech was "This is our moment," and my senior team and I challenged ourselves to "step up" to it. The phrase "This is our moment" became a mantra across the organization. The people working in Jobcentre Plus responded superbly to the extra demands placed upon them. They rose to the challenge of the moment with energy and pride, putting customers at the heart of their response.

When I joined the UK civil service in the 1970s, I was initially on a six-week contract as a temporary administrative assistant. My biggest motivator from the early days was that I wanted to help people and I wanted things to run well. I realized that there was within me the ability to make a difference and make things better.

Defining moments happen when people have belief in you. I am fortunate to have worked for a number of truly inspirational leaders. When I was reluctant to apply for promotion to the senior civil service because I didn't think I was the kind of person "they" wanted, my Director, Stephen Holt, said to me:

> What do you mean, you're not applying? What is there not to want? You are already leading 14,000 people to deliver operational services to customers in London and the South East. Those who have spent all their working lives in Head Office would kill to have your CV, and we need people like you in the senior civil service.

It was a turning-point for me.

I knew I had to seize the moment, and for me it was a life change. When I was asked to step into the role of Acting Chief Executive of Jobcentre Plus, I decided there could be no half measures. It was clear to me that from day one I needed to do the job as if it was mine. To drive through the changes, my task was to lead the organization and also to make it impossible for anyone else to be given the job! Once I had said this out loud to the top 200 leaders, I believed it myself. This was a moment of clarity when the focus of my energy became clear. We were about to embark on major and, for some people, unwelcome changes in organizational design and large reductions in our workforce; I did not want us to step back from those necessary changes.

Defining moments can come when you know you have something distinctive to offer and are holding your own. You do not always recognize at the time that a moment is particularly significant. Sometimes it is standing outside a moment, acknowledging its distinctiveness and seeing how it fits into the pattern of moments that are important.

Peter Shaw has been a valued presence at two of my defining moments. He collected feedback on me from senior colleagues, who said that I was making a valuable contribution as Chief Executive. This was a powerful moment of affirmation. I could not continue to pretend that I was there by chance.

When I was considering whether to apply for the role of Permanent Secretary at Her Majesty's Revenue and Customs (HMRC), Peter absorbed my hesitancy. His quizzical look when I suggested I was not sure I wanted to be considered for the job was part of the process of switching my attitude to a role which I now thoroughly enjoy.

Peter helped me to understand what I value in a job. HMRC is a perfect fit. Peter's book guides us through a range of moments of significance. He encourages us to stand back and recognize the importance of moments that might be surprising, joyful, angry or painful.

The book contains a rich blend of examples, ideas and practical suggestions. It will stimulate you to look for, accept and create moments of significance for you.

Peter draws from his wide experience as a Director General in government; as an executive coach working at the top level in the private, public and voluntary sectors; as a business school Professor; as a Governor at a university college and a sixth form college; and as a parent of three young people in their 20s making their way in very different spheres.

I commend Peter's book. If you are open to the idea of defining moments, reading the book could change your attitude to your work and your life. It could mean that you see new opportunities and feel more confident in your next steps. Reading the book is likely to be a defining moment for you. It could be that "this is your moment."

LESLEY STRATHIE
Permanent Secretary
Her Majesty's Revenue and Customs
London, UK

Acknowledgments

Reaching the age of 60 allowed me to look back and recognize the defining moments in my life, not all of which I fully appreciated at the time. I am grateful to the individuals who have been part of my journey and the defining moments along the way.

The book is dedicated to Frances, with whom I have shared many defining moments during approaching 40 years, which includes the time we met, got married, had three children and had the opportunity to meet a wide range of people while living in Durham, Godalming and London.

Defining moments have provided a rich theme of conversation with many individuals. Those who have particularly influenced my thinking include Una O'Brien, Ric Todd, Melanie Dawes, Adam Sharples, Nicola Shaw, Chris Trinick, Alistair Redfern, Matt Baggott, Anne Wilmot, David Bell, Stuart Senior, Helen Gosch, Jim Hughes, Claire Tyler, Fiona Spencer, Helen Judge, Nick Bowers, Hilary Reynolds, John Hogan, Tom McLaughlan, Charlie Massey, Rob Dean, Andrew McDonald, Mimi Anderson and Liz Stocks.

I am grateful to Claire Sumner and Hilary Douglas, who read an early draft of the first section and who gave me insightful comments. Particular thanks go to Zoe Stear and Mairi Eastwood, who read the full text and provided valuable reflections which helped me get the book into final shape.

Claire Pratt was politely persistent in fixing conversations with lots of people about the theme of defining moments. Jackie Tookey and Tracy Easthope were enormously helpful in typing sections of the manuscript, remaining cheerful throughout. Helen Burtenshaw was a great help in putting together the final text.

Palgrave Macmillan has been an excellent publisher to work with. Stephen Rutt commissioned the book and has always been a source of wisdom. Eleanor Davey Corrigan was full of practical advice as the manuscript turned into a book.

I am grateful to Lesley Strathie for contributing the foreword to the book. Lesley began her working life as a temporary administrative assistant in a government office in Stranraer. She is now the Chief Executive and Permanent Secretary of HM Revenue and Customs, one of the largest employers in the UK. In addition to experiencing many defining moments in her career, she has always aimed to create defining moments for others so that they are able to grow in understanding and impact. She is a superb role model for future generations of leaders.

I am grateful to my colleagues at Praesta Partners, who have always been an important source of encouragement and support in both the coaching and the writing. They are a delightful group of people full of energy and candor.

My hope is that your defining moments will help you grow in your own understanding and wisdom. Whatever your age, may there be a richness about your defining moments that continues throughout your life.

Any royalties I receive as author are going to Tearfund, which provides practical help for those living in poverty to enable them to have a future.

I thank McGraw-Hill for permission to quote from R. Charan, *Leadership in the Era of Economic Uncertainty: The New Rules for Getting the Right Things Done in Difficult Times*, © The McGraw-Hill Companies, Inc., 2009, and Eugene O'Kelly, *Chasing Daylight: How My Forthcoming Death Transformed My Life*, © The McGraw-Hill Companies, Inc., 2006. Nancy Kline graciously allowed me to list the 10 components of a thinking environment from her book *Time to Think*.

SECTION A

Introduction

Our lives are full of defining moments. But do we recognize them? Are we prepared for them? Do we understand them and build on them?

Often we are going too fast to see the significance of defining moments. Sometimes we can be too blinkered to recognize their full impact. It is often only as we look back that we see the impact of key moments in our lives.

In our work the pressure might be relentless. We are focused on one task after another. Striving to achieve targets leads to a one-track mind, and we might fail to see and enjoy moments of significance for us.

When we understand the defining moments we are going through, it helps put our work and life in perspective. It enables us to enjoy and relish those moments of significance and to move on in a constructive way from moments that might feel destructive.

Life is full of moments that matter which we might or might not recognize at the time. How do we best interpret the defining moments that matter, whether or not we recognize them immediately? How do we best understand defining moments that are changing our attitudes, beliefs and actions? The more we understand ourselves, and our reactions and how we are changing, the more integrated and responsive we become as individuals and leaders.

Living with paradoxes

To be comfortable in ourselves we have to be able to live with paradoxes:

- How can we go fast and slow at the same time so that we keep up with the pace of change and yet slow our thinking to a point where we can see a wider perspective?

1

- How can we be immersed in the here and now and also see the future so that we bring a balance between the short and the long term, between the immediate and the eternal?
- How can we both see and understand the detail that is important and see the wider context?

The enjoyment of looking at a landscape combines seeing the individual trees and taking in the breadth of the vista. How do we best achieve this dual perspective as leaders?

Central to living with these paradoxes and maintaining a balanced perspective is being confident about which are the defining moments in our work and personal life, inter-relating them coherently and then building on them for the future. Just as the bridge that crosses the estuary has a succession of stanchions rooted in the estuary bed, so our personal story of defining moments creates foundations for the decisions we make for the future and conditions our ability to see and use future defining moments to best effect.

Defining moments often occur when we see reality from more than one perspective. It is when we cross-check our view of a situation by looking through the perspective of other people that we begin to grasp what is real and what is illusory. We need to be aware of the lenses through which we view reality and how that same reality is viewed by others. Then we can more readily see the many shades of truth and live with paradoxes more easily.

Living effectively through change is in part about understanding the defining moments in our past experience, but it is also about being willing to embrace the prospect of future defining moments which will enable us to step up to take on bigger and new challenges. To thrive we need to be able to change and modify our perspective and not be stuck in a rigid and dated worldview, but at the same time we need to stay true to our core values. We need to be flexible and responsive, to view reality with detachment and creativity.

Defining moments come in all shapes and sizes. Some are dramatic moments such as childbirth, starting a new job or a being diagnosed with a major health scare. Other defining moments are very private moments of satisfaction or pain. Our lives are a cacophony or occasionally even a symphony of defining moments.

Sometimes we feel bombarded by moments we are trying to learn from. This experience can be akin to facing a barrage of questions. At other times, we long for defining moments that take us out of a predictable routine. Moments that give us joy can rush by, while moments that give us pain seem to drag on for ever. In our busyness we rush from one moment to another without savoring each moment or standing back. When we are trapped without activity that gives us energy, we can let low moments drag us downward mercilessly. We can face a welter of different moments full of varying emotions. How can we piece together these moments so that we can see a pattern and feel that life has some coherence?

In a faster, faster world we are juggling to balance work, family commitments, and community and personal responsibilities. We are conscious that the speed of life affects us in many ways:

- *Physically* we might not take the opportunity to keep as fit as we would like to or ought to.
- *Mentally* we might oscillate between focusing on pressured activity and exhaustion.
- *Emotionally* we might experience more intense highs and lows because of our work, the expectations of those around us or family and financial pressures.
- *Spiritually* we might be on a treadmill, unable to think about the purposes of our lives and how we link our personal beliefs, values and commitments.

The importance of personal stories

The following brief reflections from individuals might help you begin to think about moments that count for you. Perhaps some of these stories will resonate with you.

Una O'Brien is a Director General in a government department. She reflected on moments that count:

> It sounds like a cliché, but I really do try to remember that "this day will never come again." When things are not quite right, you have a moment to call time, you have to take that moment, speak up and act. This requires a particular awareness and self-confidence and it's a capacity I'm always trying to improve.
>
> Equally, when you're leading, you have to be able to stand back and see what's going on from a wider perspective. I like to use the idea of the dance floor and the balcony – being engaged in the action, but at the same time, knowing when to pause, take time out, observe what's going on across the piece and adapt as needed.

For Una there is a balance between focusing on the use of opportunity within the moment and marking and enjoying defining moments.

When I was asked to run a workshop about defining moments for a group of senior leaders, these were the factors they concluded were most important:

- Being fully present in the moment
- Seeking not to have avoiding moments – and when they happen, trying to understand why and to use that understanding construct-ively
- Being open to surprise
- Always celebrating milestone moments
- Working through the significance of moments when you deferred to others (i.e., did you defer for a good or a bad reason?)

What was most important for this group was the combination of being fully present and at the same time understanding their own reactions, whether of celebration or avoidance.

Ric Todd, the UK Ambassador to Poland, talks of the importance of creating moments that work for you and understanding your own rhythm. He comments:

> Having a systematic approach to creating defining moments works for those who like using a plan. But for a lot of people when difficult issues come up they tend to park them, wait for their instincts to help deal with the issues and not address them systematically. Under-standing your own preference is, therefore, so important. Oliver Cromwell used this technique, which he called, "be still and wait upon the Lord."
>
> A regular routine helps. Being on automatic pilot can release the brain to have time for reflection. But it is important to link together the value of the routine alongside the beneficial effect of doing things differently and looking at issues from different perspectives.
>
> Sometimes a defining moment is choosing not to do something. That can be just as important as deciding on a particular direction of travel or the setting of a new objective.

The learning from Ric is the importance of getting the right rhythms and being clear on your objectives; it is also about being willing to rec-ognize that a defining moment can be when you choose to say "no" to a particular avenue.

Henry holds a leading role in a major private sector consultancy organization. For many years he had felt a bit hard done by. He had progressed well in his chosen career, but he did not enjoy the work or his progression as much as he had hoped. There was a defining moment when the chip on the shoulder went. He comments:

> There was a moment when I really began to believe in myself. I am now much more open-minded and realistic.
>
> Running the marathon set me off on the right course when I joined a new organization. In preparing for the marathon I set out a plan with milestones. It demonstrated to me that I can do things I think are not possible if I set out clear steps. It was deeply personal for me. No one else was alongside me. It was only me who knew what the training, the race and the outcome were like. It felt to be a fantastic achievement.
>
> I now believe in myself much more. I know I can do difficult things. The chip on the shoulder has gone for ever. There is genuine self-belief coupled with knowing that I must keep being open-minded and must keep learning.

Where do we begin?

Do any of the following perspectives resonate with you?

For John: "Life is so busy: there is no time to stand still. If only I could hold on to good moments in the working day, I would have perspective and energy for the rest of the day. I am not good at recognizing defining moments that are working well for me. I need to be able to treasure good moments and ensure that I embed the learning from them to the best possible effect, so that I can keep up my energy and juggle all the responsibilities on me at work and at home."

For Marion: "Looking back there are key defining moments in my life and work that have been so important. It was a particular conversation that set me off on a new direction or the comment from my teenage daughter that encouraged me to think in a new, more confident way about how I am tackling a difficult situation at work. The challenge for me is recognizing more readily when defining moments are about to happen and how I use them to understand myself and my situation better."

For Sarah: "There were defining moments like joining a new team or moving to a different workplace which I only partially understood the significance of at the time. There have been challenges that I have not faced up to, where a minor problem has become a major issue. If only I had stood back, seen the problem more clearly and defined in my own mind what I should do, then the situation would have become a moment that defined me in a new and constructive way and not have been a source of damage to my confidence and reputation."

For Roger: "I was rushing around spending too much time exhausting myself. I was trying to solve every problem at work. A wise colleague sat me down over coffee and helped me slow down and reflect on the values that are most important to me. I needed someone to force me to do quiet reflection. I now do that more often and it helps me get issues into perspective. The challenge for me is keeping up that quiet reflection and enabling others to be able to do the same."

This book aims to help you stand back and make sense of key, defining moments in your work and your personal life. My hope is that it will enable you to live in the moment more effectively and to piece together the tapestry of defining moments you experience.

The demands upon you are considerable. You want to make the most of both your opportunities and your responsibilities. You want to learn from others how to stretch good moments and survive through difficult moments. You want to recognize and use moments of truth more effectively. Sometimes you see the significance of events dimly and want to be much sharper in recognizing and responding to realities.

You treasure key moments in your life; you want to capture the moment, but you have to keep moving on because of the pressures of life. There are joyful moments, creative moments and milestone moments. How can you treasure these good moments so that they provide energy for the future? How can you create a rhythm of moments for the future which will mean you use your time and energy more effectively?

Life at work and at home is very busy. Your brain is having to go faster and faster; you are having to cope with a wider range of pressures. It can often seem that life is out of control and there is no time to stand back. How can you ensure your time is used ever more effectively? You keep hearing about time management and keep trying different things, but most of them fail. Focusing on your defining moments will enable you to develop a clearer framework about who you are, what matters most to you and how you want to use your skills, experience, time and energy.

Many of us feel deep frustration about our inability to create rhythms in life. An effective rhythm comes from understanding the moments that have been most important to us in the past and then creating a pattern for the future which brings and conserves energy, uses our intellectual strengths to best effect, understands and works with our emotional needs, and resonates with the personal or spiritual values that are most important to us.

The journey through the book

This book will take us on a journey through:

- *Living in the moment* so that we recognize the significance of light-going-on moments, milestone moments and surprising moments
- *Stretching the moment* so that we are able to stand back and get maximum benefit from positive times
- *Surviving difficult moments*, whether they are down moments, crisis moments or moments of anger
- *Treasuring the moment* so that we make every moment count, recognize moments of truth and embed learning moments
- *Capturing the moment* so that we make the most of creative moments, can grip the moment when action is needed and can live with discord
- *Creating future moments* so that we can focus in the moment, build a rhythm of moments that works for us and create moments of learning and hope for others
- *The way forward*, which is seeing the pattern of moments and the next steps

My hope is that this book will enable you to piece together your catalog of defining moments in a different way. You might more readily see a pattern from the past and develop a clearer expectation for the future. You might be less concerned with your emotions of the day and see your work and life in a wider perspective.

You will be equipped to see future moments in a different way. You will more easily relish joyful moments at work and at home. You will cope with setbacks in your career with greater detachment. You might be both more focused and more compassionate. My aspiration is that you will enjoy work more and feel you are living life more abundantly. Reading this book might affect your physical, intellectual, emotional and spiritual wellbeing, so be ready to be surprised!

The ideas in this book have been strongly influenced by the experiences of a first career in government and a second career in executive coaching and writing. I have had the privilege of working as a Director General in government, as a Partner in a private sector organization, and in various leadership roles in the voluntary sector. I am indebted to the many people I talked with as I developed the ideas in this book. I hope that the book stimulates your thinking in new ways. My aspiration is that you will view your future pattern of physical, intellectual, emotional and spiritual moments in a new way and will be stimulated to bring an open, creative and fresh perspective informed by your previous experience but not blinkered by it.

The book can be read right through, or each of the chapters can be read and reflected upon separately. Each chapter includes examples and practical reflections encouraging you to take greater control of your own moments while always being willing to be surprised. Each chapter ends with five suggestions about next steps as prompts for further thought. So, do enjoy the book and the many defining moments that you will experience over the years ahead.

Peter Shaw
Godalming, Surrey

SECTION B

Living in the moment

This section is about living in the moment so that we can make the most of every moment and not be continually burdened by concerns about future events or what might go wrong. It focuses on:

- Light-going-on moments
- Milestone moments
- Surprising moments

Each chapter starts with a paragraph summarizing its overall theme, followed by an individual's story. As you read through the chapters, you might reflect on where you are in relation to each of the themes. What is your experience, and what might your next steps be? This might mean being more explicit about light-going-on moments, more structured in thinking about milestone moments and more open to surprising moments. This section aims to encourage you to understand the significance of past moments and to be entirely present in the moments you are living through.

1 Light-going-on moments

A moment when the light goes on could be when you realize or accept that you have the ability to do something you had not previously thought possible. It is when new confidence bursts through and you see a situation or your future in an entirely different way. What was hidden in the shadows is now illuminated, and the path ahead becomes clearer. It is like the light at dawn, which brings a fresh understanding and clarity about the way forward. It can be a joyful realization or the recognition of a painful reality.

Helen's story

Helen had always been academically bright and had passed through school and university at the top of her class. As a graduate entrant into the business world, she made good analytical contributions, but she lacked confidence in informal settings and was not good at networking or building relationships. She felt that her influencing skills were minimal. She was unsure whether she could cope and be successful in a big corporate organization.

Gradually, as she got to know people, she spoke her mind more readily. She began to see that she could make influential contributions. One boss was explicit in demonstrating his belief in her and encouraged her to speak her mind more and more. Those around her saw her as influential, but Helen was still inclined to view herself as an 18-year-old who lacked confidence rather than as a 24-year-old with a bright future.

It was the clear feedback from a senior member of the company that made the biggest difference. He said to her, "You need to believe in yourself more: you have tremendous potential, but it will lead to success only if you can believe you are influential." It was a powerful message delivered sensitively and thoughtfully. "Yes, that is me: I am going to believe in myself" were the words Helen repeated to herself as she jogged her favorite route early one morning.

Six years on she looked back to that light-going-on moment when she accepted the wise counsel that she should believe in herself. This moment was crucial in building her confidence at work; it was the point when her career took off.

This chapter is based on various examples of individuals talking about light-going-on moments. I encourage you to reflect on which of these resonate with you.

Doing it my way

Fiona talks about the importance of recognition from others when you have made difficult things happen. The recognition that "I did something difficult and it worked" is a powerful endorsement. She says:

> Looking back on difficult problems you have sorted out gives a great sense of accomplishment. It is an affirmation of your values when your approach works, for example delegating effectively to key individuals and not doing it all yourself. The defining moment is when you are comfortable saying, "I am going to lead this organization my way."

For Fiona success was a combination of building a sequence of successful outcomes and then recognizing that her contribution was distinctive. She looked back on an occasion when she had intervened and changed the direction of a piece of work. She had done a quick sense-check on some figures which she thought were misleading but which everybody else thought were secure. She ensured the figures were sorted out quickly by asking key questions, bringing in independent specialists to look at the figures and giving steers about what needed to be examined. The realization that doing it her way worked was based on her confidence about asking good questions. The light-going-on moment was based on knowing she had the ability to ask the right questions, which gave her the confidence that leading her way would be effective and would carry people with her.

Overcoming indecision

When you are in the midst of difficult choices or lack clarity about your contribution, there can be light-going-on moments when the path ahead becomes clearer, sometimes in an unexpected way. Ronald tells a story about the time he was asked to join a major national organization as Chief Operating Officer. Initially he was not sure he wanted to accept the role, and he felt paralyzed by indecision. He was going to give a speech to a conference of those regulated by his organization. When he got there he heard the conclusions of the work that the delegates had been doing. He had expected to have to berate them for mistakes in the proposals they were putting together. The light-going-on moment was realizing that lots of positive things were happening that could be built on collaboratively. So he chose to start his speech by reinforcing the positive in what the delegates were doing and building up their confidence to tackle the areas they were obviously finding difficult.

The approach Ronald took worked well, but the practical lessons were not just for the delegates. Ronald was telling himself about the importance of being positive and believing we can be passionate in taking forward change. His positive approach to the delegates immediately converted into a new attitude to the job he had been offered. It helped crystallize in his mind the idea that if he entered the job constructively and passionately, he could make a major difference. He accepted the role and led major change successfully and more collaboratively.

For Ronald the light-going-on moment resulted from his changed attitude to the delegates, which fed straight back into his attitude to the job he was being offered. An experience in a parallel event can sometimes give us a new perspective on an issue we are wrestling with elsewhere in our working life. The light switch might be in a different room, but it casts a new light in a dark space.

Saying no

A light-going-on moment for some might be when they say "no" and the world does not collapse around them. Barbara was the Chief Executive of an organization with a demanding Chair. The Chair was pressing strongly in a particular direction and wanted action to be taken. Barbara gave clear advice that this action should not be embarked upon; her view was not popular, but she was convinced in her judgment that she should not be apologetic, and eventually her view was accepted. She recounts that as she continued to express her view, "The light bulb got brighter and brighter." She was becoming ever more confident in her own judgment and willing to be robust in defending it. It was a symbolic event for her and marked a major step-change in her confidence.

Saying "no" requires that we are sure of our ground and have enough credit in our key relationships for people to take our "no" seriously. The ability to say "no" with conviction and to explain our reasons carefully can provide a valuable light-going-on moment in terms of confidence in our judgment.

I am a grown-up now

When Marcia took on a new role she was uncomfortable when she did not know the answer to every question: she was concerned about treading on eggshells. We worked through the importance of establishing peer relationships with key individuals in which she felt confident in her own contribution. We talked about recognizing that:

- By virtue of her role other people would want to talk to her
- Because of her knowledge people would want to engage with her and listen to her
- After only a few weeks in the job she knew far more than other people about key subjects
- She had the ability to influence the outcome of conversations: simply building up the quality of a relationship with a key stakeholder was an adequate outcome in itself; there did not have to be revelations or amazing new conclusions

Becoming grown-up for Marcia was about recognizing that she did not need to know the answer in every conversation; a good engagement could involve working through the issues and getting closer to the answer. It meant not being overawed by somebody's authority; it involved discussing issues on equal terms.

Marcia concluded that grown-up conversations involved:

- Getting to a point where you are talking about a shared problem
- Being explicit about when you think others are making a good point
- Playing back the learning from the dialogue
- Thinking what it would be like to be in the shoes of the other person
- Recognizing the importance of continuing to build up key relationships over time

Marcia had been used to a world where she got on top of things very quickly. She was now recognizing that in a demanding role she would not know the detail of everything, but that progress comes through being credible and engaging. You do not have to be perfect or all-knowing to be a grown-up leader.

The light-going-on moment for Marcia was when she came to believe that she could operate on equal terms with very senior professionals and recognized that she brought considerable knowledge and experience to the table. She was able to engage in constructive dialogue with positive outcomes and was delighted by her progress and the jump in her confidence.

Knowing a conclusion has to be reached

Melanie, a Director General within the UK government, talks of a defining moment when she was dealing with the Chief Financial Officer of a major organization. There had been serious negotiations without any conclusion being reached. The light-going-on moment was realizing that she was in a position to cut through the issues and reach a conclusion. She knew that a way through had to be found. What mattered was recognizing the key facts and uncertainties, knowing how much they were worth worrying about and then going for a negotiated outcome with the CFO. At the end of the day it was going to be her decision. The light-going-on moment was recognizing the nature of her authority and not drawing back from the responsibility that she faced.

Leaders grow in authority when they recognize that the buck stops with them when it comes to reaching conclusions, whatever sphere they are in. A light-going-on moment for a head teacher, a medical consultant, a banker or a CEO can be when they accept and feel comfortable with the responsibility of taking final decisions.

Rewriting our own rules

Sometimes we can be caught in the grip of one set of procedures. We see life from one career or professional perspective. We might not appreciate how blinkered we have become. Perhaps we have been on one pathway and have not begun to think seriously about moving in a different direction.

Rupert had done accountancy work since leaving university. He had dabbled in buying and doing up property but had not thought seriously about moving into this area as a second career. His current accountancy job was coming to an abrupt end, but his mindset was that he had to stay in accountancy. When he talked the options through with a friend, his passion grew for developing his property expertise and moving away from what now seemed dull and lifeless in accountancy. As he talked through the options he became more and more passionate and could see the practical steps he should take.

As a result of these conversations Rupert concluded, "You have given me permission to rewrite my rules for my own next steps." There was a point in the conversation with his friend when Rupert's eyes lit up: he had broken out from the rigid strictures of his previous thinking and was now working through ideas about the future in a far more constructive way. There was a new excitement because a light had gone on.

Recognizing that sometimes we can write our own rules and not be bound by the strictures or expectations of others can be a profound light-going-on moment. This is not about an unrealistic notion that the world can be dramatically changed; it is about the recognition that you can determine your future pathway more often than you think.

Next steps

I encourage you to reflect on light-going-on moments that have been powerful for you. They might have been about doing it your way, over-coming indecision, saying "no," recognizing you are grown-up now, realizing that a conclusion needs to be reached or accepting that you can write the rules. Light-going-on moments are not just for an instant. They make a permanent difference to the way we look at the leadership we bring and the wider contribution we make.

Some practical questions to reflect on:

- Which two or three light-going-on moments have been most import-ant in my leadership journey?
- Could I have celebrated the effect of those moments even more?
- Have I fully embedded in the approach that I take the lessons from those light-going-on moments?
- What light-going-on moments do I continue to look for?
- What helps me know that a light-going-on moment might be about to happen?

2 Milestone moments

Milestone moments are times when there is new clarity. Sometimes milestone moments come together; at other times they might well be strung out. Milestone moments might be about clarity of direction or communication. They could be about knowing yourself better, changing your attitudes, knowing your patterns and recognizing the effect of words of challenge. Milestone moments might result from difficult times following a stepping up of responsibility or accountability. It is often only in retrospect that we recognize the significance of particular milestones. Significant milestone moments might happen only a few times over an individual's working life.

> ## Ernest's story
>
> Ernest had drifted into a career after receiving a reasonably good degree from an established university. His boss recognized the potential in him but was not convinced that he could bring enough determination to succeed.
>
> Ernest's boss began to work with him on particular milestones. Step by step Ernest's contribution started to increase. A report was well received by the Board. He chaired his first major meeting with an external stakeholder. He represented the organization in an important negotiation with a outside body. He went for a bigger job and was successful in his application.
>
> For Ernest there were a sequence of milestone moments that made a huge difference to his confidence and his personal impact. He was drifting no longer and beginning to make his mark. He was indebted to his boss for working with him to set a series of attainable milestones.

Clarity about direction

Many people have defining moments when they become clear about their sense of direction. These moments might come after a period of uncertainty, or an external shock might reinforce the need for a new clarity.

James had gone into a new job. In his previous role his self-confidence had been undermined. He had scored himself 3 out of 10 in his former job on self-confidence, but a few months into his new job he was scoring himself 6 out of 10, with the aim of reaching 8. Three months into the new job he knew he needed to be clear about his sense of direction. He decided that he needed to create a milestone moment when he could articulate to himself what he had learned in the role and what his next steps were going to be. He wrote down:

- Five key learning points from his first three months
- Five strengths he brought to the role
- Five things he wanted to achieve over the next six months
- Five ways he was going to ensure he kept focused on those objectives
- Five things he was particularly going to enjoy about the next six months

He used this script with himself, with a good friend and with his boss. He was more confident about his next steps after articulating key points that mattered most to him. He felt that he now had a clear sense of direction and was on course for his confidence to reach 8 out of 10.

James had created his own milestone through the discipline of writing down key points. He felt confident this approach would work for him and experienced a great sense of relief and accomplishment when he had agreed his next steps with his boss.

The first step toward reaching clarity about our sense of direction is honesty about our own confusion and lack of clarity. The next is putting stakes in the ground, which might be evidence affirming the capabilities we bring alongside clarity about what we need to deliver. Establishing these fixed points can give us the freedom to think about different approaches to delivering our objectives and about what will give us joy in working through these approaches.

Clarity about the way we communicate

Milestone moments are not only about what goes on in our head; they are also about how we communicate effectively to others. Adam Sharples, a Director General within the UK government, talks of a conference in the 1980s that completely altered his attitude to writing. He was at a workshop led by a subeditor from *The Financial Times* who demolished the language of this group of academics. She said communication was about clear, honest expression. The more complex the idea, the more work you need to do to express it simply. Many people hide behind obscure language because they fear their ideas will look less impressive if they are set out in simple terms.

For Adam, in his work as a civil servant, the risk of creating obscurity rang true. The lesson from the subeditor was the importance of bringing simplicity of expression. Her message was about honest and clear communication, clear impact and simplicity of expression. This milestone moment has had a profound influence on Adam's career; the tests of simplicity and clarity have become central to any decision he is responsible for communicating.

Milestone moments might well be about recognizing clear, simple truths and then communicating them effectively. They are about not allowing our lack of clarity or muddled thinking to deflect us from a relentless focus on clarity and simplicity when we communicate complex messages.

Recognizing that you have stepped up

In my book *Raise Your Game: How to Succeed at Work*, I suggest that stepping up effectively depends on a powerful blend of:

- *Self-belief* that comes from a combination of inner confidence and clarity of values
- *Practical action* that is realistic, determined and planned

I suggest that stepping up depends on a balance between being and doing. *Being* is about being comfortable in your skin, whatever role you are in. *Doing* is about the practical behaviors and steps that underpin success.

Amanda wanted to ensure that the away-day for her directorate was a success. She wanted the members of the directorate to be less tentative and more deliberate. To this end, her main concern was to demonstrate to her people that she believed in them. Staff survey results had been good, so she knew that she had a strong foundation on which to build. She handled this event by:

- Spelling out the big-picture issues
- Allowing her inner resolve to show through
- Bringing self-disclosure in terms of what she was learning about herself and her impact
- Describing some of her own thought processes in reaching decisions
- Reinforcing the importance of communication
- Sharing different approaches to communication with her staff

She felt increasingly comfortable in her role as the leader, and it showed. Because she was confident that she had stepped up successfully into the role, others followed her and became more confident and effective. The away-day marked a major step forward for Amanda and for her directorate. It was a milestone moment because both the leader and the team knew they had stepped up successfully.

Sometimes individual events can provide a stepping-up milestone. Celebrating and looking back can reinforce the importance of a milestone. On other occasions a milestone is a shared recognition of the challenges ahead and a joint resolve to move on and tackle them successfully.

Accepting words of challenge

Sometimes a key milestone moment is when we accept some words of challenge and allow ourselves to respond in a more wholehearted way than we had anticipated. Anne Wilmott holds an HR Director role in a leading health body. When she was young, school was not a very fulfilling place for her, and she left education with limited qualifications. She comments:

> One of my defining moments was when I decided to go back to study and got a place at university studying part time for a degree. I was the oldest in a group with lots of under 25s who seemed to know everything. After two weeks, knowing there was a waiting list, I spoke to the course leader about giving up. He looked me in the eye and said, "Fine, I will give you a week to consider. Then if you decide to give up, go away and waste the rest of your life. You have the biggest case of cold feet I have ever seen. Are you going to take the easy way out?" That was nearly 20 years ago but the words still sting. I probably have his words to thank for building a career. I came out as the top student in the group!

Anne tells a story about another milestone moment that came from a direct challenge. A boss once said to her that she was the worst delegator she had ever come across. Anne's reflections were:

> She had nailed me. She had topped me. It was a hard thing to hear. I was really hurt. Then I accepted I was not doing the job I was meant to do. I recognized the strength of the message. It was a milestone for me in the way I used the skills of my staff.

Sometimes we avoid challenging conversations or dismiss them. We often think that challenges are ill founded or that we are a victim of circumstance and therefore the challenge, even if correct, is still unhelpful. How can we best use personal challenges as a means of redefining our approach and allowing our response to a challenge to be a milestone in the way we approach issues or use our time and energy?

Knowing ourselves well

We keenly observe other people, but how often do we observe ourselves? Sitting outside ourselves and seeing how we respond to different situations can give us new insights. Knowing ourselves is not about indulgence; it is about being realistic about what works or does not work for us and allowing ourselves the luxury of not feeling guilty about our foibles.

Ken had been observing himself taking on a difficult leadership challenge. He articulated the changes that he had observed in himself:

- I am saying "no" more often.
- I am bringing emotion from a more detached position: this is about bringing passion but not being controlled by it.
- I understand how to build commitment from others more readily.
- I know more accurately when my energy is going to drop, and I am better equipped to do breathing exercises and ensure short breaks so that I can rebuild my resilience even in the most demanding of times.
- I recognize that I don't need to be leading from the front all the time; enabling others to lead is even more important.

There are moments of insight when we understand ourselves better. They might involve reflection after a series of difficult meetings. They could come following feedback in a performance review or feedback from a psychometric exercise. That willingness to stand back and accept who we are and how we have responded can provide a powerful milestone moment in terms of developing the robustness to cope with future shocks.

Changing attitudes

Howard had been a loyal servant to his organization. He had covered a senior role for a couple of years, and then the organization had brought in a new person to fill the post. He felt demotivated and undervalued;

he felt the organization had not taken into account any of his feelings. He felt that people were being disrespectful and rude to him. He had seen himself as part of the bigger family of senior leaders, but it was now evident that this was not the case. It made him realize that he was much more on his own than he had thought. He recognized that he had been overworking and had lost a proper sense of priorities in his work and family life. The benefit of this shock was that he was now in a different place. He commented:

> I needed to change my life. The way I deal with people is different. I am much less concerned about how people judge me: this is much less important to me now. Whereas all the focus used to be on work, now I am a lot more conscious that there is more to life than this. I am reading a lot more. I am out a lot more doing different things. There is more diversity in the types of moments I enjoy.

The result is, paradoxically, that he is enjoying his job much more and is probably being better at it. The milestone moment for him was about changing his attitude. The result was a new lightness of touch and much more pleasure in his work.

Milestone moments are not always about action; they are often about attitude. When I am asked to name the most difficult decision I have taken, I say it was changing my attitude toward a couple of individuals. Some attitudes can be so deep-seated, based on our previous experience of an individual, that we find them difficult to change. But there can be a sense of liberation as we move on from an attitude that has held us captive.

When I was working in the civil service, my wife, Frances, would say that I had a milestone moment every six months. When I had got reasonably established in a role I would say, "I've got it. I understand what I am doing now." For each of us there is a pattern of milestone moments that are most important to us. Understanding that pattern can help us predict and understand future reactions and enable us to avoid the angst of uncertainty that can so often beset us.

Accepting words of praise

We are often bad at paying each other compliments. Bland words of thanks rapidly feel like insipid wallpaper. The most effective words of praise are specific and are linked to particular contributions or pieces of work.

Within our families we often take each other for granted and do not bring enough personalized expressions of warmth and endorsement. In some father-and-daughter relationships certain difficult aspects of the teenage years can linger, with the intimacy between father and daughter not being as overt as it might be.

Milestone moments in work and family life can be about clear, specific words of praise and thanks said genuinely with no ulterior motive. Honest expressions of praise can have a profound impact on other people's confidence and enable them to move into an even more effective working or personal relationship. Milestone moments are about emotions as well as facts. They are personal as well as professional.

Next steps

We have explored a range of types of milestone moments. With each of them there can be a sense of progression. We might not recognize the full significance of each milestone moment at the time, but as we look back we can see a pathway that has helped us grow into the person we are. As we look to the future, seeking out milestone moments can have a profound effect on our personal growth and destiny.

Questions to reflect on might be:

- Which milestone moments have been the key stepping-stones for me?
- Am I able to articulate those milestone moments clearly and simply to others?
- Which milestone experiences have helped me step up most successfully in both confidence and competence?
- Which words of challenge have been major milestones for me?
- Do I know myself well enough to be able to interpret future milestones accurately?

3 Surprising moments

Surprising moments come in many ways. Good surprises can encourage us and give us new energy. Bad surprises can knock us off course. Success comes through enjoying good surprises and not just rushing on to the next task. Keeping bad surprises in perspective and accepting they will happen can help us respond in a way that is constructive and not undermining. Being prepared for surprise is about openly accepting whatever life brings and having a thick skin when we are faced with shocks that would otherwise unnerve us. Being able to smile at surprises and be philosophical about them is central to our wellbeing.

Clare's story

Clare lived a busy, demanding life, with her job, her home and her three children filling up most of her time. She was focused in everything she did and was always generating lists. She was remorseless about delivering on her objectives. Clare was an achiever admired for balancing so many things at the same time. She had generated her own predictability: she knew when the children would be happy or upset. It all ran like clockwork, but then surprises began to happen: her boss became unpredictable, the children became ill, and her husband became irritable. It was all getting her down, and she was feeling tired and low. She was not getting to the end of her lists. It felt like one bad surprise after another.

What turned things around? Her daughter kept hugging her. Her boss said "Thank you" on a regular basis and meant it. Her husband recognized that his approach was not entirely helpful and as a peace offering gave her some plants that burst into flower. Gradually, Clare began to enjoy life outside the office. A sequence of pleasant surprising moments had begun to raise her spirits. It was a fragile transition, but enjoying surprising moments helped take her in a positive direction and lifted her gloom. Clare began to see the bad surprises and the good surprises linking together. This difficult period prepared her to cope more equitably with bad surprises in the future. She was going to treasure good surprises even more as she knew how important they were to keeping her equilibrium.

Spending three days in a game reserve taught Frances and me how to look for surprises. In the reserve we were on the lookout for joyful surprises, while being equally conscious that we could be surprised by a venomous snake or a cheetah. Because these wild animals did not appear to order, we were both diligent in our observation and ready to be surprised. We never did see a cheetah, but we were ready to be surprised by one!

What have been our good surprises?

Our lives are littered with good surprises we have forgotten. The surprise might have been a high exam mark, a job offer, words of praise from a colleague or a hug from a friend. We so readily forget these surprises and just move on.

When my elder son was 25 I offered to take him to a city for a long weekend as his birthday present. He specified a city in the former Eastern Europe but wanted the location to be a surprise. I managed to keep the destination a secret until the announcement at the departure gate that the flight to Berlin was ready to board. The father-and-son trip was extra-special because the destination was a complete surprise to Graham.

Harvey talks about good surprises that have been important in his career in the finance sector. He is conscious of the competitive nature of the world in which he works. He is grateful for people's encouragement and was touched when he was strongly supported after making a silly mistake. Harvey had expected to be criticized but was reassured by words of support from his boss, who admitted that a similar thing had happened to him. It was a pleasant surprise to Harvey that there could be such humanity and support in so competitive an environment.

Jane had taught generations of children and was now Head Teacher at a school on a demanding housing estate. The pressures seemed relentless. She had coped with many grumpy and taciturn teenagers. Whenever these individuals came back two or three years later happy and enjoying student life, it was their words of thanks to Jane that cheered her. She was surprised and pleased that they bothered to come back. Their thanks meant a lot to her: she had taught herself to enjoy them and not just pass them off as part of the job.

Which surprising moments have you most enjoyed? Do you allow these surprising moments to affect your enjoyment of life? How good are you at enjoying surprising moments and ensuring that good surprising moments do not unnerve you? For the future, might it be helpful to look at positive surprises, write them down or internalize them when they occur, and find every excuse to celebrate them with your family and friends?

What have been our nasty surprises?

Nasty surprises happen. All the best intentions and careful planning will not mean the end of unpleasant surprises, but can we prepare for them? An unpleasant surprise might be a diagnosis from a doctor, the termination of our employment, the ending of a friendship, criticism from a colleague or a budget that does not balance.

I was not prepared when it was announced in 1995 that with immediate effect the organization where I was HR Director was going to be combined with another organization which also had an HR Director. It was inevitably a disappointment when I ceased to have a seat on the Board for a year, but in retrospect it set me off in a new direction, with no regrets. Although I was surprised by the announcement, I was always 100 percent committed to making the merger of the two organizations a success. This commitment ensured I had no temptation to wallow in resentment about the surprise. I was clear that the merger was the right next step, and this helped minimize any downside of the surprise.

Brian had worked loyally for the same big corporate organization for 20 years. He had always had positive performance reports, but the effect of a recession was that senior staff numbers were going to be cut by 30 percent. Although this move was not entirely unexpected, it still came as a nasty surprise. It was a matter of Brian waiting to see whether he still had a job in the organization. His family and friends became even more important to him. He knew that one way or another the next few weeks were going to be decisive. Either he would be re-establishing his position at a senior level in the organization or he would be moving on. He tried to keep his cool, but it wasn't easy.

What unnerving surprises have you experienced? How well do you cope with bad news, and how do you minimize the negative effects of bad news on your wellbeing? Perhaps recognizing that negative surprises will happen regularly can help, as can observing how others respond in such situations. It can help to reflect on the good that can come out of nasty surprises. Seeing negative surprises as an inevitable part of your life's story can keep you feeling reasonably in equilibrium.

Living with surprises

As you look back, can you allow yourself to be surprised by your own life? This is not indulgence; it is a way of confirming how you have responded to opportunities and circumstances. It might be worth reflecting on what has surprised you most about your life's journey so far and what most delights you about your personal learning over your life.

We might not look back positively on every occasion when we have been surprised by ourselves. There will have been moments when we moved from being emotionally in control to being emotionally out of control, when we took advantage of someone's good will, when we were blinkered to our impact on others or when we were short-sighted and self-serving. Welcome to the human race!

We live with our paradoxes and inconsistencies. These moments of being surprised by our own failings are as much a part of us as more positive surprises. Feeling permanently guilty about these negative surprises does us no good at all. It is not a matter of blanking them out; it is about recognizing that they are part of us and then moving on with a new sense of purpose and compassion. Moving on might involve building a new relationship with those we have wronged, without killing them with kindness if they do not want it.

Is it worth reflecting briefly on times you have surprised yourself by actions you are not proud of. What was the cause of these negative surprises, and what is your key learning about yourself as a result? Are you content with the way you handled moving on?

Surprising moments do happen

For 27 years Nelson Mandela was incarcerated and Apartheid looked to have a permanent hold on South Africa, yet in 1990 Mandela was released and addressed a huge crowd from the balcony of the town hall in Cape Town. Four years later he became President of a reinvigorated country. No one had expected this outcome 10 years earlier. In 1989 the Berlin Wall came down; a decade earlier the Warsaw Pact had seemed a permanent barrier to democracy.

Whatever seems fixed and unchanging can crumble. Whatever now seems a rigid barrier can come down, whether it is political, professional or personal. Where there are unacceptable limitations on fair trade, restrictions on employment or relationships blocked by a wall of anger, there can be moments of change that take us by surprise. Looking back and reflecting on moments in recent history that surprise us can be a stimulus to thinking about how we want to influence change in the future to help generate positive change.

Hazel was not looking forward to early retirement. As we talked though some of the enjoyable surprises the next phase of her life could bring, she moved from apprehension to anticipation. So much so that when she was offered the opportunity to stay in her job longer, she declined, saying that she was now looking forward to the surprises in the next phase of her life.

There will be limitations on the time and resources available to us, but are there opportunities to seek out surprises? At work, this might involve doing activities outside our comfort zone, visiting different locations or trying to understand our competitors more. In our personal life, it might involve visiting new places, talking to new people or going to a different type of film or play. There might be someone whom we have always regarded as intensely boring. Can we seek out their wavelength and see how we can find out something surprising about them to make conversation with them a pleasure and not a pain?

It might be worth reflecting on:

- What you might do to open up new surprises in your work and in your personal life.
- How you can take forward an activity in which you are ready to be surprised.
- Whom you might spend time with, ready to be surprised by a sense of shared discovery with that person.

Be surprised about whom you can work with

Most of us prefer working with like-minded people, yet we often recognize that our most creative working relationships are with people who are different from us. Roger was given the challenge of working with a colleague as the joint head of a major initiative in the private sector. They talked about the gifts they would bring to each other and how they could complement each other's skills and style. Roger was clear from his previous experience that collaborative leadership required shared goals and agendas, good communication, a similar work ethic and a recognition of and respect for differences in background and approach, with any disagreements being handled immediately through quickly convened meetings.

Roger was pleasantly surprised how well the arrangements worked even though there were marked differences in approach. Success came through careful planning, not having expectations which were too high and working out carefully the process through which disagreements would be resolved.

Previous experience had taught Roger not to be too rigid in his thinking about whom he was going to work with. It had taught him to be open-minded about applying different leadership arrangements effectively. He was pleased that his willingness to experiment had worked. He would try joint leadership again with individuals with whom there was an even greater degree of difference.

Living with serendipity

Stuart Senior held a range of senior posts in the private sector before becoming Chief Executive of ELEXON, which is at the heart of the British electricity wholesale market. He sees serendipity as important. When he was visiting his parents many years ago, he saw a *Sunday Times* recruitment advertisement for consultants at Deloitte Haskins & Sells. Attracted by the pen picture, he applied for the position. He was successful, and in five years he was made partner. A few years after Deloitte merged with Coopers & Lybrand, Stuart handed in his resignation, which required a year's notice, as he was in danger of getting bored. He saw an experienced headhunter, which led to a very different role at Centrica, before he moved on to Marks & Spencer and then to ELEXON.

For Stuart, serendipity is about being open to new things, being willing to go with the flow sometimes and not getting worked up about what you cannot influence: shape what you can fashion, and let the rest go. Serendipity is also about seeing things coming early and deciding when to exit an organization on your own terms, even if at the time there are no obvious opportunities for influence, progression or, above all, personal growth and development elsewhere.

Our attitude to surprise or serendipity will depend in part on our personality and in part on our life view. Whether we think that life is a sequence of random events or that all things work together for good, keeping our mind open to change means we can experience good surprises, but blinkering our approach is far more likely to lead to bad surprises.

Finding nuggets of truth

Even in uncomfortable situations, or when we experience the most negative of surprises, we can find nuggets of truth. Nicola tells a story about attending the funeral of a family friend. The preacher's style and voice wound her up. His preaching grated, but she remembered him saying, "We walk through the valley of death." In one sense it was a negative and discouraging tone for the funeral of a much-loved lady. But the message that stuck with Nicola was this theme: "You have to walk." The nugget of learning was the importance, whatever the situation, of keeping walking. If you are scared, you have to make progress a little at a time. If you are joyful, you can bounce along more contentedly. But you must keep going.

The learning from Nicola's experience was that however negative a surprise is, there will often be a nugget of truth. The bad surprise might stay as a painful memory, but it might be mitigated by a nugget of learning that is precious for the future.

Be ready to be surprised by your unconscious learning

Many of us experience occasions when we are unable to think our way through a problem and so we give ourselves time to reflect on it. We park it in our mind, and by the following morning we have a solution. This might be in part because by the following morning we are fresh and alert. But our unconscious mind might have been working overtime linking together different bits of our experience and putting the problem into a wider context.

When we can see no way forward, experience tells us that parking an issue and sleeping on it can be the best next step. However we describe this process of unconscious thinking, allowing it to happen and accepting the results can be a relief and can provide pleasant surprises.

We know that unconscious thinking does not always solve problems. It does not take away the need for hard analysis. But it is part of our armory, and it is foolish to dismiss its significance. It might lead to surprising outcomes we never anticipated.

Next steps

I encourage you to look forward to and enjoy surprising moments. Whatever they are, so be it. When they are positive, celebrate!

May I suggest reflecting on:

- Which surprising moments do I most treasure?
- Which surprising moments have I learned most from?
- How willing am I to be open to surprising moments in the future?
- How well prepared am I for surprising moments that are discouraging?
- What is the most recent surprising moment that has had a big effect on my attitude to my work?

SECTION C

Stretching the moment

This section is about stretching the moment so that there is opportunity to reflect and enjoy moments that are important to you. It looks at:

- Standing-back moments
- Joyful moments
- Making time go slowly

My purpose in this section is to encourage you to stand back and get the maximum benefit from positive times. We can rush through life and not give ourselves enough time to stand back, to be joyful and to stretch out good moments. My encouragement to you is to be explicit about creating standing-back moments, to enjoy good moments and not feel guilty or inhibited about doing so, and to stretch out those good moments for as long as possible. Time rolls relentlessly on, but we can sometimes influence the sense of pace and push the pause button.

4 Standing-back moments

A standing-back moment is when we pause and take stock. It might be a time when we look to see a wider perspective. We might be viewing the events of the day against a longer timescale. Standing back might include looking at dilemmas from the perspectives of different people. Standing back can be a time to observe whether our personal drive is taking us in a positive or a dangerous direction. Standing back can also be about pausing, taking breath and letting our unconscious do the thinking. It can include observing our emotional reactions to different situations and using that input as valuable data.

Bernard's story

Bernard was always very focused. He led his team well; he and they were always task oriented. Bernard had a strong track record of delivery; he was clear what he wanted and set out to achieve his targets with tremendous energy.

But he caused considerable irritation to other people. Colleagues did not always think that he listened to them. They regarded him as far too single-minded for his own good. His approach tended to create conflict and was often counterproductive. His boss was forever having to unblock problems and was beginning to lose patience.

After Helen observed Bernard having yet another difficult conversation with a colleague she decided she needed to take action. Fearing that she might get her head chopped off, she said to Bernard firmly but politely that his approach was sometimes counterproductive. He needed to cool it and stand back a bit and not be so relentlessly focused on his own objectives. Bernard looked resistant to this message, but in his heart of hearts he knew that his pride got in the way of adjusting his approach.

That weekend Bernard went for a long walk and thought through some of his attitudes and approaches. He knew he needed to see his priorities in a wider context. He recognized that he needed to stand back a bit more. He resolved to build stronger relationships with some of his colleagues and a stronger consensus about shared objectives.

The following week, much to the surprise of his colleagues, he encouraged some joint conversations about shared objectives. He was calmer and more reflective following his long walk. This greater emotional ease was immediately mirrored by his colleagues, and they reached agreement on a way forward. There was a step-change in the constructive relationship between Bernard and his colleagues. He was so thankful that he had been willing to stand back and go for that long walk.

This chapter looks at aspects of standing back through the eyes of different individuals.

How have I grown?

One key element of standing back is to turn around and see your journey over recent years or months and take the time to see how you have changed. It is about bringing clear objectivity in looking at those changes and allowing yourself to be pleased by what you observe.

Gordon had been in a much bigger job over the past year. At the start it had been tough, and sometimes he had felt out of his depth. On occasions he had thought of himself as the junior partner, but gradually Gordon had become more established and confident. Gordon had been reluctant to review his progress, but eventually he was happy to take stock. He described how he had grown as a leader:

> I have become much less daunted. I am more confident in using the "I" language. A lot of things are feeling easier than they did. There is lots of evidence that "I can do it."
>
> I am now making big asks of people and it is working. I am not overawed by my colleagues and am working constructively with them. I am less fazed by people I do not instinctively understand. I have recruited key people to be my champions through building mutually supportive alliances.

Gordon was increasingly focusing on the things only he could do, on the strategic impact he could have and on getting the right relationships in place to ensure delivery happened. He was more liberated in his approach because the feeling daunted dimension was much, much less. As Gordon stood back and reflected he became ever more confident in his own contribution. He was able to celebrate the growth that he had observed in himself and to be more confident in looking to the future. Time spent standing back was crucial to embedding his learning and becoming more confident in his judgment for the future. Key words of affirmation from Gordon were:

> I am much more confident. I can distil and pick out the nub of issues. I can grow a picture and perspective about what needs to happen. I can increasingly trust my hunches. I am much better at adjusting my approach. I am much clearer about how best to manage people. If anything is thrown at me I can create a vision for the future. I am much better at listening and learning.

It is a useful exercise to stand back and look at your journey over the past year. Key questions to ask yourself can be:

- In what ways have I become more confident in my judgment over the past year?
- How has my impact increased in different settings?
- To what extent are other people trusting and using my skills and expertise more effectively?
- What are the top three things that I have learned over the past year?
- How am I ensuring that I am embedding that learning?

Taking stock with others

Sometimes the standing-back reflection can be done alone effectively. On other occasions we can benefit from the challenge or companionship of others. The views of a boss can be damaging if they detrimentally affect our confidence or stimulating if they take us to another place in terms of our self-confidence and personal insight.

Ideally the views of the boss are communicated directly to the individual. Often a third party – a mentor or a coach – can help draw out a frank set of views from a boss and then use that information constructively to help the individual move positively into a new space.

George was very affirming about the contribution that Roland was making. George was clear that Roland had a sound intellectual grasp, understood how to work with partners, was capable of wielding influence and was not fazed by the different aspects of the role. But George was also clear about key development areas for Roland, including keeping focus on raising standards of performance, making an increased contribution to corporate leadership and not holding back when he was clear about next steps.

George and Roland benefited from having a time of standing back to look at Roland's development. Providing a quiet space and enough time for a reflective conversation was crucial. Roland needed to leave the conversation confident of his relationship with his boss and clear about his next steps, knowing that his boss would both challenge and encourage him.

Is there a risk that we sometimes restrict the number of opportunities to obtain feedback from a boss or someone else we work with? Receiving good-quality feedback is a precious gift. Seeking quality feedback is not about self-indulgence or wanting praise every week; it is about building a clear frame of reference for your capabilities and seeking robust and constructive data to enable you to continue to grow in confidence and effectiveness.

Reframing reality

We can get stuck in a mindset which limits our ability to stand back and reflect. A strong focus can turn into blinkering when we fail to see what is happening around us. Sometimes we can view the world in a much more positive way if we reframe how we describe the reality we observe. For example "change" might seem a negative word with connotations that unsettle us. Replacing the word "change" with the word "improvement" can make us feel much more positive and more conscious about reaching constructive outcomes. The key challenge is how we frame a positive perspective that is genuine not illusory. As soon as we begin to fabricate a potential positive outcome we are at risk of self-delusion, but a robust emphasis on what might be is a powerful driver of success.

Alan was conscious that he often felt frustrated. He wanted to turn his frustration into a constructive rather than a destructive use of energy. Whenever he felt frustrated about an issue he began to think through what he believed in and what he could feel passionate about in that area. He knew that if he could turn his frustration into a passion for change he could motivate himself and keep himself positive. The extent of his frustration might well mean that he couldn't reshape the whole project, but if there was an element of the project he believed in, he would be able to motivate himself to make a positive contribution to the whole project.

What was key for Alan was understanding his frustration, knowing how it affected his attitude and behavior, and then being able to park that frustration as he thought through what positive contribution he could make that would keep him motivated. He knew the frustration would still be there from time to time, but he now knew he could live with that frustration when there was clarity about how he wanted to contribute.

When you feel frustrated in a particular area of work is it helpful to consider:

■ What are the causes of the frustration?
■ To what extent can that frustration be limited in its scope and impact?
■ Where within this overall activity can I identify a contribution I can make that I can be passionate about?
■ What aspect of the project or activity do I strongly believe in which can provide motivating energy that keeps the degree of frustration in check?

Stock-taking through observing others

One use of standing back is to observe others and articulate what you are learning from others. Amanda reflected on her experience of working for Zoe. She was conscious that Zoe chaired meetings well, provided a broad perspective and could be very influential in certain contexts. But Amanda also observed that Zoe sometimes made things difficult for herself by being too focused and becoming immersed in the detail. Amanda observed in Zoe that by virtue of her relentlessness she could turn potential defeat into success and was opportunistic in sometimes taking ground when others were focused elsewhere.

Amanda was able to articulate those attributes she admired in Zoe and those she was less sure about. She knew which aspects of Zoe's approach she wanted to embrace and which she wanted to be wary of mirroring. Amanda was conscious that because they worked closely together she was very likely to be embracing some of the approaches, both good and bad, of Zoe whether she liked it or not.

It can be well worth standing back and reflecting on the leadership style and impact of people you work with. Questions to ask yourself about somebody you work with might be:

■ What do I admire about their approach?
■ What do I think is counterproductive about their approach?
■ What do I want to embrace or not embrace from their leadership style?
■ Am I aware of the extent to which I am mirroring both the individual's strong points and less strong points?

Reassessing your approach

Moments of standing back can embrace looking at how we have grown, observing others and reframing our perspective. We are all creatures of habit. Sometimes we can get upset when external changes mean that our routines will no longer work. The skill is to use external change as a good moment to reassess our approach. When there is a change of boss this can mean reassessing what has worked well or less well and thinking through the right approach with the new boss. When we move from one job to another it is taking stock of what has been successful in one role and considering how our approach could be different in a new role.

When Jane was reflecting on her learning from the experience of working with a new Chief Executive she said:

> I am both more comfortable and assertive at the same time. I recognize that I am a strong activist who is learning how to reflect. I am watching when I become intellectually lazy. I am tutoring myself to stand back in the moment so that I am consciously recognizing what I am thinking about and what I am worried about.

For Jane it was important to take stock and assess the impact on her of working for a new boss and think through her own learning. She had considerable abilities and was becoming ever more confident in the use of her time and energy. She recognized that she needed to reassess her approach regularly without becoming too self-indulgent.

Relevant questions for us might be:

- How open am I to reassessing my approach?
- Which aspects of my leadership approach am I becoming more comfortable with?
- Am I self-aware enough to be able to know what is working well or less well?
- Am I able to view reassessing my approach as a strength and not a weakness?

The value of routine reflection

For many people in the western world there used to be a weekly cycle in which Sunday was a day when the pace was slower and there was greater scope for reflection. The demands and choices of modern life mean that many people do not have a regular routine which allows time for reflection. If time for reflection has to be consciously planned on a daily basis it might never happen. If time for reflection is built in as part of a routine it is less likely to be eroded.

Time for reflection can follow different cycles. It could be the annual long vacation, the quarterly setting aside of time for reflection, the monthly stock-take with a coach or mentor, or the weekly review of progress and reflection for the future.

William was in a busy Chief Executive role. He was being pushed hither and thither by different influences. There were contradictory pressures from different stakeholders. His staff were creative but sometimes inflexible. He knew he had to give a strong and clear lead. What was important for William was finding opportunities for reflection. For William these opportunities were a combination of having a monthly conversation with a trusted coach, allowing himself a "thinking day" once every four months, and reflecting on a Sunday evening about what had gone well during the previous week and where he wanted to focus his energies for the coming week. He was conscious that if he did not have these moments of reflection priorities could get out of kilter. Investing in himself and his own space was absolutely central to his using his time and energy effectively.

Key questions for you might be:

■ What sort of pattern of reflection works for me?
■ How do I create regular thinking time for strategic and longer-term issues?
■ How best do I reflect on a weekly basis and renew my energy and focus for the coming week?

Allow yourself to be forced to think in new ways

We are sometimes forced to stand back whether we like it or not. External economic and political change can mean that our role becomes redundant or that if we do not change significantly it will rapidly become redundant. Sometimes we have no option but to go with the flow and then be ready for a moment when we can step back and see where the flow has taken us.

Within local government in England the Chief Education Officer was once the prime mover in the leadership of the Local Education Authority. Now it is the Director of Children's Services, reporting to the Children's Services Committee, and the scope of the work is the range of services for children and not just education. Those individuals who have responded well under the new arrangements are those who have been willing to think differently about their responsibilities, who have embraced the focus on linking services together and who are not focused on only one specific area such as primary education or social care.

When Chris Trinick took on a change leadership role at Lancashire County Council he could see much more clearly than he had done before the potential for joining up services. He started to link achievement in schools with what the local authority was doing on housing and health. For Chris it was a defining moment when he saw the opportunity to link services together and took this opportunity forward constructively. What might have been a threat now became a big opportunity.

When we are forced to think differently because of economic or political change, is our natural reaction to see this as a problem or as an opportunity? Changes can mean that what was previously not on the agenda is now possible. Questions to ask ourselves can be:

- How well do I respond when I am forced to think differently?
- How could I more frequently see external change as an opportunity rather than a problem?
- How excited do I allow myself to become by impending change?

Standing back to let others grow

Standing back might not be something we do for our own benefit. It can also be about enabling others to grow and move into space we previously occupied. Many leaders talk about the breakthrough when they accept that they do not have to do everything themselves. Robert talked of the joy of seeing people grow when he had moved into a Chief Executive role. He talked about removing constraints from operational leaders to enable them to lead change effectively, standing back when you have set a clear direction and letting individuals into the space, enabling members of your senior team to believe that helping each other to be successful is important and focusing continually on influencing people within your team to challenge and encourage each other.

Standing back might sometimes involve biting your tongue if someone is learning from experience and needs to get some things wrong. Knowing when to stand back and when to engage might well not be easy, but it is central to success. You will not get it right all the time.

Key questions to ask yourself are:

■ Am I standing back enough to let others take decisions?
■ How can I become more comfortable in standing back when I know that I would not take action in quite the same way as those now in the lead?
■ How can I demonstrate to myself that I am using the standing-back time well?

Next steps

We have looked at different aspects of standing back. I encourage you to ensure that you have standing-back time. It is essential to build in a pattern of standing-back moments in a way which fits your personal context and personality. It might seem selfish to create standing-back moments, but it is essential for your long-term wellbeing.

Questions to reflect on might be:

■ When am I at my best in terms of standing back?
■ Which types of standing-back moments do I need to ensure are firmly in my diary? How much of this time is me alone and how much is with others?
■ What type of interaction with others helps me stand back effectively: is it talking to a friend, conversations with a coach or a chat with a colleague?
■ What do I observe from others who use standing-back time well?
■ What further standing-back time am I going to build into my diary?

5 Joyful moments

Joyful moments are to be treasured. They might be moments that are instantaneous and unexpected. They might be moments of celebration or success after a long period of hard work. Joyful moments can be ecstatic, or they can be quiet times of inner satisfaction. So often we feel that joyful moments are transitory and we rush on to the next thing without fully enjoying moments of pure joy. Joy cannot be turned on like a tap, but we can create situations which either encourage joy or limit its likelihood. We can be joy's best friend or its biggest skeptic. I want to encourage you to see moments of joy not as indulgence or as escapism but as times of special significance which are to be treasured, remembered and repeated.

Jeanette's story

Jeanette had a tough job as a hospital consultant. The routine was relentless. She had to be engaging with so many people, and the patients placed demands on her time and energy. She sometimes felt pushed around by her colleagues. There was no time to do anything other than work, work and work until she went home exhausted at the end of her shift.

Jeanette knew that she needed to find ways of lifting herself and making herself smile. There were glimmers of joy when she gave good news to patients or she was thanked by patients and their families. But there was always that temptation to rush on very quickly. She knew she was doing a good job, but she did not give herself the scope to enjoy her own professional success.

It was a close friend who said to Jeanette that she needed to slow down and take some satisfaction in what she was doing. The friend encouraged Jeanette to describe the positive reactions from patients, the thanks from her students, the respect in which she was held by the nurses and the personal satisfaction of a job well done. As Jeanette began to talk through these words of thanks and praise with her friend she began to smile. Yes, she did believe these comments were true. Yes, she could allow herself a moment's satisfaction. Yes, it was OK to smile and feel an inner glow. The message from Jeanette's friend was to hold that good feeling, not to rush on to the next thing, and to revel in that sense of joyful satisfaction. Jeanette began to accept that being joyful was good for her and not a waste of time. Jeanette's promise to her friend was to keep ensuring that there were joyful moments in her working day.

Being able to find joyful moments is primarily an attitude of mind and is about the company you keep. It is about seeing the positive in difficult roles, celebrating success, seeing and remembering joy in the day-to-day, enjoying liberation moments and step-change moments and remembering to smile. It is about hearing the crickets and recognizing the freshness in life.

Seeing the positive in demanding roles

Whatever the task or pressures, we will see the problems. We can, to an extent, condition ourselves to see the opportunity for joy as well as the risks and threats. To what extent can we develop a mindset whereby we look for incidents or conversations that will enable us to see the positive and provide a source of encouragement?

Paul had had a series of demanding jobs; he was not viewed as having been very successful and had been required to take on a role at a more junior level. Initially he felt cross, misunderstood and unhappy, but he recognized he had little option. He still had a job and the opportunity to renew his reputation. Thankfully he could view the future in a more positive light than he had feared. Even though the job was not of the status he wanted, he could see the opportunity it provided.

Paul was now heading a much smaller department than he had been responsible for previously. His pride had been dented, but he could see the scope for tackling some difficult problems successfully and reaching some outcomes which would mean that customers were served much more effectively. He surprised himself by how excited he became about this opportunity. He moved on more quickly than some of his friends, who were still feeling resentment on his behalf.

Questions we can ask ourselves might be:

■ How readily do I see the positive in demanding roles?
■ What might give me joy even in the most demanding of situations?
■ Can I believe that in any situation there will be moments of joy?

Celebrating success anyway

Many leaders I talk to admit that they are not good at celebrating success. Often this is because they are so driven that they want to move on to the next task. Even after a major project has been completed they will allow themselves 10 minutes to have a quick celebratory drink, and then it is on to whatever is the next major task. The result is that their staff can feel their contribution has not been properly appreciated. These bosses do not intend to limit or constrain the celebrations of their staff, but the behavior of rushing on to the next thing can be a dampener and can result in a reluctance to work for the same boss again. Limiting celebration can have a detrimental effect on building strong teams for the future.

Some leaders are reluctant to celebrate success because they are fearful that pride comes before a fall. They see a risk that there is bound to be a catastrophe if they allow themselves to celebrate. This is not a logical cause and effect, but it is a fear in the minds of many leaders. The corrective is sometimes the voice in our head saying, "Don't be so silly." A practical way forward is to recognize that there will always be risks of failure and that these are not increased or reduced by having moments when you celebrate success. Arguably the risk of failure is reduced if celebrating success creates motivation that leads to the right outcomes.

In a busy operational business there are always things going wrong. But if the manager focuses only on what is going wrong, there can be a downward spiral in energy and commitment. The good manager will say, whatever is happening, we must find a means to recognize what is going well. Even if the economy is difficult there must always be some good things to celebrate, such as the personal development of an individual or a qualification someone has received. Success comes through finding moments to celebrate, whatever.

Enjoying liberation moments

One of the strongest focuses of my coaching work is encouraging people to identify moments of liberation and then mark them. Liberation can be about moving on from previous constraints or attitudes. When an individual moves into a bigger job there can be a sense of liberation from previous responsibilities. When an individual is in a more senior role there is the opportunity to be liberated from doing some of the detailed work. As an individual gains in experience and begins to trust their intuitive judgment more they can become liberated from having to master every point of detail.

Liberation is often about not feeling you have to live up to other people's expectations. It is about not doing what you think you ought to do but moving on to do what you think is the right thing to do in a particular situation. Liberation is about playing your full part as a leader on a corporate Board and not feeling you are constrained by being a junior member. Liberation can bring a powerful sense of freedom and of having your own voice.

Rachel had been in the shadow of some dominant leaders. She had learned a lot from them but wanted to run her own organization. At long last she had the opportunity to head her own directorate. She took with her a lot of the learning she had gained from her previous bosses, and she was determined that she was going to lead her directorate her way. She knew the values that were most important to her. She wanted to set the right tone about visibility in the organization. She placed strong emphasis on meeting and learning from people right across the directorate. She felt both a sense of liberation in her leadership role and indebtedness to those people who had taught her so much in previous jobs.

Questions that you might ask yourself are:

- Do I feel a sense of liberation in my current job?
- What would need to happen for me to feel a sense of liberation?
- How best can I use the sense of liberation that is available to me in this role?

Enjoying step-change moments

Andrew had been through some tough times. He had been very close to one boss, who had moved on. There was a great deal of change and uncertainty, but he knew he was stepping up in confidence and moving into a new space. There was lots of learning for him about stepping up which gave him a sense of personal satisfaction and joy. He was not taking things for granted. He was recognizing that if there were disagreements, they were not personal. He was measuring carefully the amount of emotional energy he was putting into particular issues. He was recognizing the importance of not displaying anger and of controlling situations effectively. He had developed the technique of encouraging other people to talk to enable him to think through his own next steps.

He knew from the reaction of others that he was in a much better place. There was a sense of positive energy which came from a growing reputation and his own self-discipline in terms of the use of time, energy and emotion. He was becoming kinder on himself. He was not having to justify his own existence. He was saying "no" to some things where he might previously have said "yes." He was pacing himself much better and allowing himself to feel a sense of joy as he stepped up to take on bigger responsibilities.

Stepping up can create a sense of burden and responsibility. But it can also lead to a strong sense of satisfaction and the knowledge that you are making good progress and are now able to deploy the full range of your abilities and experience to wider effect.

Seeing and embracing joy in the day-to-day

Joy is not just about big successes. It is about enjoying joyful moments of many types. These moments might be incidental, but they can still provide powerful memories. These moments of joy can come from many different aspects of your life. As a stimulus to thinking about the types of moment of joy to remember, may I share with you the following personal examples. As we arrived at Hambledon Church in Surrey on a glorious Sunday morning, one of the older parishioners said, "You can hear the stillness." That sentiment was absolutely right as we stood and listened. Because of the warmth we didn't need to move. The quietness in the air produced a deep, warm stillness which enabled us to smile with a sense of joy and then move into the church.

Ed was a widower who was marrying again at the age of 60. On his stag day, 11 of us set off on an early-morning train to the Isle of Wight and got shouted at by a grumpy old man for being too noisy. The stag day had been organized by Ed's son; it was a special day for him as he was about to be best man at his father's wedding. As a group of sober guys in our 50s (plus two people in their early 20s) we enjoyed peaceful walks through the Isle of Wight countryside, the hectic fun of the dodgems, wine tasting at a vineyard and the spices of a Malaysian restaurant. As we traveled back, with the sun just setting as the catamaran came into Portsmouth harbor, there was a feeling of relaxed companionship and joy. We were companions with Ed as he was about to enter the next phase of his life. It was a treasured day that we remember often.

When I walked Hadrian's Wall in northern England there were many different types of joyful moment. As I walked east from Carlisle, fertile valleys gradually gave way to moorland and then rugged crags. Each phase was distinct. I walked gradually through the landscape, and yet every couple of hours or so I was conscious of being in a very different topography. There was a joyful spring in my step as I recognized that the steady walk was traversing a wide and varied landscape. It was one dramatic crag after another, each with its own distinctive character. The route along Hadrian's Wall seemed to be almost vertical in places. The surprising element was that my energy levels were highest on the difficult terrain. There was a sense of achievement as I topped each successive crag. I was no mountain goat, but I got there.

On the Hadrian's Wall walk, joy came through unexpected conversations. At one bed-and-breakfast establishment there were four men in their 60s walking the Pennine Way whose conversation was full of jollity and teasing humor, there was a family from Europe who kept themselves to themselves but were enjoying their own company, there were a couple of Americans who were mesmerized by the history and were lapping it up, and there were three people in their late 60s who seemed to have done all the major long walks in the UK. It was the variety of the walk that created so many moments of joy, from the bird sound to the unexpected rustling in the undergrowth, the refreshing feeling from a welcome cup of tea and the companionship of fellow-walkers.

Enjoying joyful moments at special events with your children creates a set of pictures which will be long remembered. My daughter's graduation day in 2006 was full of special moments. Ruth had not enjoyed her first year at Lancaster University and had transferred into the second year at Royal Holloway. Part of the graduation day for Ruth was a sense of fulfillment that she had stayed the course and reached her destination. It had not been an easy road, which is why graduation was so special. There were photographs, laughter, hugs and a wonderful sense of accomplishment. The graduates were the centre of attention and were quite rightly celebrating their moments of success. There were uncertainties about the future for many of them who were still looking for employment, but this was a moment to savor. At an evening celebration, 14 of us from different areas of Ruth's life met for dinner. There was laughter and companionship. The day created a set of joyful moments long to be remembered.

It can be well worth creating your own litany of joyful moments from different aspects of your life. Whether you capture them in photographs or in stories, I do encourage you to let them live and be re-told at regular intervals. This is not indulgence; it is allowing the richness of life to flow through your whole being so that whatever the pressures at work there is a stream of moments of joy that you long remember and that keep you feeling that many aspects of life are good.

Questions worth asking yourself are:

- What are the small moments of joy that are very special to me?
- How do I keep building up those personal moments of joy?
- How best do I relive those moments when encouragement is important to me?

Remember to smile

One question I often use in coaching conversations is "What gives you joy in a particular situation?" Often someone will say, "I cannot see what will give me joy, but I can see what will make me smile." Allowing yourself to smile in any situation is half-way to giving yourself a joyful moment. Sometimes it is smiling about the absurd; sometimes it is imagining that a difficult meeting is taking place on top of an iceberg rather than in a dingy meeting room. It might be allowing your sense of the ridiculous to lift your spirits when you are feeling intensely bored.

One of the virtues of smiling is that other people respond and do the same. We mirror each other's behavior often, so smiling is good for us and for other people as well. This is not about encouraging trite grinning. It is about allowing the human dimension to show and celebrating the ability to laugh.

Deborah and Bob were facing a difficult decision about whether Deborah should take a job in another part of the world. They were sitting in a field talking through the possibilities. As they relaxed and talked they heard the noise of church bells; they could hear the crickets. Deborah said, "I think I am going to be offered the job." Her husband said, "I know you are." It was a golden moment; all their senses were engaged. They were totally at peace with the environment and with themselves. There was clarity of vision. They smiled, and they knew what their next steps would be.

The recollection of that joyful moment was so strong that it provided a sound basis for working through their next steps, none of which have been easy. That moment of listening to the crickets and smiling provided a point of affirmation. The picture in their minds of that joyful moment hearing the crickets gave a security about the next steps which was important to them.

Next steps

Do keep remembering and celebrating those joyful moments. They can be moments when decisions are crystallized, when there is an affirmation about the next steps, when there is a sense of bonding and togetherness which can provide a strong foundation for the future.

Questions to reflect on might be:

- Do I allow myself to seek out joyful moments?
- Do I create joyful moments for myself and others?

■ Do I allow enough time for the celebration of joyful moments?

■ How can I be more of a catalyst for others in enabling them to create and enjoy joyful moments?

■ Which are the joyful moments I will most remember from this week?

6 Making time go slowly

It is an undisputed fact that there are 60 seconds in every minute, 60 minutes in every hour and 24 hours in every day. But our perception of the speed with which time is passing varies widely. Sometimes joyful moments pass quickly, while boring moments can take an age. Are we just at the mercy of time and our perception of how quickly time is passing, or can we be more firmly in control of how we use our time and how quickly time seems to pass? Sometimes success seems to depend on making time go more slowly so that we can complete the tasks we need to do and create moments of stillness within our days.

Asif's story

Asif was always watching the clock. Life was hectic in the big trading room. He was conscious that the expectations of him were huge in terms of what he delivered. He needed to be alert all the time so that he was ready to do trades. He was desperate not to let people down. He knew that if he made a careless error it could lose the bank thousands of pounds.

The pressure kept him on tenterhooks: he could not allow himself to relax at work. The consequence was that he got more and more tense and edgy. There were disagreements with those around him because they sat so close together. He kept imagining that they were all battery hens clucking to the tune of the bank's drive to maximize its profits. He oscillated between a focused determination to make money and a sense of cynicism and even disillusionment.

He knew he couldn't go on like this. He was exhausted by the evening and would wear himself out by the age of 45. But what could he do? He was on a relentless treadmill. He knew he had to slow himself down a bit. He was conscious that he had to pace himself better and prioritize more effectively. He could not continue at this absurd, relentless pace. He began to walk a little more slowly when he went for a cup of coffee. He gradually prioritized his time and worked a bit more carefully. He knew when he was going to get edgy and cross and began to control his emotions, and because he was pacing himself better he found relationships with his colleagues more constructive. In an unexpected way, slowing himself down had enabled him to work more effectively with others.

   Making time go slowly is about both how we use time and our attitude to it. It is about varying our pace depending on the hill we are climbing and the people we are with. It can be about preparing for and savoring moments, taking difficult step slowly, taking time when difficult things hit you, building bridges effectively, using moments constructively when you are stuck and ensuring you set the pace you want.

Preparing for and savoring moments

Alistair Redfern, the Bishop of Derby, talks about the art of enabling people to have good moments and then reinforcing those good moments as reference points. There is a special skill in preparing for and savoring good moments and holding on to them so they do not dissipate too quickly. Alistair sees a dangerous preoccupation with bad moments in contemporary times. The *Big Brother* TV fascination offers a goldfish bowl of bad moments, and the art of therapy can be about focusing on bad moments. But the art of enabling people to have good moments, savor them, build on them and make them go slowly is crucial for our wellbeing in demanding times.

   Frances and I reached the age of 60 in 2009. We built into the year a whole sequence of celebrations, including celebrations with friends in two different parts of the country, three long-distance walks and a visit to New Zealand. Preparing for and then savoring each moment made our 60th joint birthday celebratory year very special and has given us a springboard for the next decade of life.

   By putting in place different events and savoring them we were making our 60th birthday last for months. For me it was a perfect example of making time go slowly when you want to enjoy, and keep enjoying, reaching a particular milestone.

Taking difficult steps slowly

In the early 1990s I was asked at the end of one week whether I would be willing to become the Government Regional Director for the North East of England on a two-year loan, and I was given until the following Monday to reach my answer. I had three days to decide. Thankfully it was over a weekend, so there was time to talk with trusted others and with the children. What was most important was that there was potential value for Frances out of the move. Over the weekend the possibility of Frances doing a postgraduate degree at Durham University grew as an attraction. That weekend was about creating space to talk and reflect so that Frances and I were at one when I said "yes" to the move to the North East. It was an important decision, but because we were able to take it slowly over the weekend it did not seem to be an overwhelming one.

Deirdre was conscious that when important decisions needed to be taken they needed to be broken down into blocks and time given to each component. If a decision needed to be taken within a couple of days rather than a couple of weeks, time needed to be created so that there was no sense of rush in making the decision. When major decisions have to be taken in half an hour there is still time to slow down and possibly have a brief time-out to allow space to reflect before rushing into a firm conclusion.

Mary was gifted at ensuring that decisions were taken at a pace she thought was right. She was willing to slow down the decision-making process when questions still needed to be asked. She was good at flagging up when a firm decision needed to be taken so that people were prepared and not taken by surprise. Mary kept her colleagues informed and knew the pace at which they were willing to make decisions. She sensed accurately when other people might want to bounce her into a decision and was clear she would never let anybody push her into a corner.

In my book *Making Difficult Decisions: How to Be Decisive and Get the Business Done*, I suggest that good decision-makers bring a balance of clarity and conviction. In terms of clarity they are looking at the facts and being utterly objective. In terms of conviction they are bringing their insights, experience and intuition to bear. Balancing clarity and conviction effectively requires that we create time and slow down time so that the interplay between clarity and conviction can take place both overtly and in the unconscious mind.

Questions to ask about taking important decisions might be:

- What is the pace that works best for me when taking difficult decisions?
- How best can I set aside time to take difficult decisions?
- How do I ensure that there is a slowing-down period before a decision is finally made, even if the overall time for reaching a decision is constrained?

Taking time when unexpected things hit you

We can plan as much as we like, but the unexpected will hit us. We can focus our energies on delivering the outcomes that we are paid to deliver. But life is not that predictable. Economic, political and personal events will surprise us.

How do we ensure that we are not thrown by the unexpected? Good risk analysis is fundamental, both in our jobs and in our personal lives. Thinking through risks can help us prepare for the unexpected, even if the unexpected event was not previously thought of. When the unexpected happens, one crucial attribute is not to get caught in an emotional response that sees disaster everywhere. When we are hit by the unexpected, success comes through slowing down the pace, putting the event into a wider perspective and gradually building a picture about what to do next. Coping with the unexpected is not about putting our head in the sand; it is about recognizing that life is like that. Major surprises will hit us, but we can choose our own reaction.

Just as an athlete has to train in order to run well, reacting well when the unexpected hits us requires forethought and preparation. This is not about glib answers that can come from trying always to think positively. It is about recognizing the reality that we can be hit by shock or misfortune and have the responsibility and the capacity to develop responses which are measured and practical.

Questions to ask yourself in preparing for when things hit you might be:

- What is my natural reaction? Is there a risk I go into panic mode, head-in-the-sand mode or paralyzed mode?
- In what ways might making time go slowly help me cope with unwelcome events?
- How can I best prepare myself to cope with future unexpected events, building in enough time to reflect in a detached way?

Building bridges effectively

Sometimes it is a matter of going slowly to go quickly. Quick decisions require trust and understanding among key individuals. Building up trust can take time; it can be a slow process to build up mutual understanding and a shared perception of the facts, but that investment will pay dividends in the long term. Building a foundation of key relationships effectively can have a profound influence on the eventual outcomes.

Building bridges across different interest groups can be a painstaking process. Creating a situation in which there is a genuine win–win for all parties is never straightforward. Bridges can be built at many different levels: the bridge could be a shared intellectual understanding, agreed priorities, an acceptance of the best way to work together or a recognition that shared endeavor can be more creative than individual effort.

Building partnerships in any sphere of work or personal life is painstaking and then highly rewarding. Slowing time down to ensure effective investment in partnerships is an effort that is hardly ever wasted, but impatience to succeed can often get in the way. What might help you best slow down your expectations so that partnership is built effectively? The answer to this question can involve realism about what is possible, patience in taking discussions forward and acceptance that sometimes partnerships work and sometimes they don't.

Using moments when you are stuck

There are moments when we get stuck and need help, but do we always recognize when these moments are happening? If we are stuck it might mean parking the issue for a while, talking to trusted colleagues, trying to find another angle or recognizing that the time is not yet right for a response or decision.

The feeling of getting stuck can lead to a sense of dejection or desperation. When you feel stuck the same messages go round and round in your head. It is as if the needle on the record has got caught in a scratch and the tune is repeating itself again and again. The relentless playing of the same line of the song might seem to go on for ever, even if it is only for a brief moment. When we are stuck, time can drag out; we need someone to lift the needle off the record and give us breathing space. Often the only person who can do that is us, after we recognize that we are stuck.

Hazel was conscious that she had got stuck: she had a fixation that the right way to approach a particular issue involved asking someone to leave the organization. Other colleagues were unconvinced, so there was an impasse. It appeared to her that her colleagues became ever more inflexible as she became increasingly adamant that her way forward was the only one that would work.

Hazel became more and more emotional inside and was in danger of being unprofessional in criticizing her colleagues. It was a good friend who recognized the impasse and encouraged Hazel to think inside the minds of her colleagues to understand why they were approaching the situation in the way they were. Gradually her perspective began to become more flexible. Hazel could begin to see some possible compromises and was open to trying out different approaches. At last she felt that she could have a constructive discussion about different options. Quite rapidly a new approach was agreed.

How conscious are you of getting stuck and becoming inflexible? What helps you take time out to look at a problem through different lenses and reach a more ready acceptance about a way forward?

Keeping time going slowly

Time is like an ever-rolling sea; it is relentless and demanding. In the modern world of 24/7 activity is it futile to envisage time going a shade more slowly? Are we captive to the pace of life we are part of, or is there something we can do about it?

We cannot change the 24/7 world, but we do not have to be on the rollercoaster all the time. Can we put in fixed points so that time does go a bit more slowly for us?

Jenny was about to move into a big new job. We talked about a sequence of fixed points which would help her keep her life under control. She was going to:

■ Work a nine-day fortnight, which meant working longer hours on nine days and having one day to catch up with domestic activities.
■ Ensure that part of her journey to work was a vigorous walk.
■ Aim to get away from the office at 6:00 p.m. every evening, even if she did a bit of work on the laptop later in the evening.
■ Be alert if people began to delegate tasks upward to her.
■ Be selective about the number of things she took on.
■ Watch the expectations from others so that not too many time demands were place upon her.
■ Ensure that her discussions with key stakeholders were constructive but not excessively time-consuming.

The approach Jenny planned to adopt was to aim to give people quality rather than quantity time. She saw the key skill as giving people her sole, undivided attention and then moving on effectively to the next conversation or piece of work.

Derek had always seen business and stillness as two opposite states of being. Business was what you did at work. Stillness was what you did at the weekend or on holiday. The revelation for Derek came when he began to think of shafts of stillness within a busy day. He began to see the brief walk in the park, or the purchase of a cup of coffee, or the walk to another office as a lung of air that helped him enable time to go a shade more slowly so that his energy was refreshed. Creating stillness was about small periods when he could either empty his mind or fill it with something completely different so that he could return to activity in a new and refreshed way.

Next steps

Time is a precious asset which we can make go more slowly or more quickly. Developing the gift of slowing time down is precious whether we are making decisions, coping with the unexpected, building bridges or moving on from being stuck. Success is about controlling time rather than time controlling you.

Questions to reflect on might be:

- How much control do I really have over my time, and what are my choices?
- How can I best create time to take difficult decisions?
- How much time am I willing to invest in building long-term partnerships?
- What have I learned from moments when I have been stuck about how to use time effectively?
- How can I create moments when time goes slowly during busy days?

SECTION D

Surviving difficult moments

This section is about surviving difficult moments. These moments can have a profound long-term effect on us. They might, at the time, feel overwhelming, but they are often the moments that shape us more significantly than any others.

Difficult moments come in many guises. It might be a difficult situation or business problem. It might be a personal difficulty of which others are unaware or only dimly aware.

We look specifically at:

- Down moments
- Crisis moments
- Moments of anger

For all of these moments there is a balance between being fully immersed in a difficult moment and ideally being able to observe your attitude, actions and behavior in that moment. It is about bringing detachment and self-awareness about your own attitude and behavior. This will often mean not being too hard on yourself and being able to laugh at your idiosyncrasies.

7 Down moments

Down moments can be times when you lose authority, when you feel burdened, when you live with dark moments or when you feel stuck or beat yourself up. Down moments are a fact of life and often are among our most formative experiences. Often it is down moments that make us the people we are. We have to live with our own frustrations, but sometimes we have to stop beating ourselves up and move on. Living effectively with our down moments is one of the most important requirements for moving on successfully as a leader. Cherishing the way we overcome down moments is a special part of our self-recognition.

James's story

James seemed to take one blow after another. He was very conscientious as a university lecturer but never seemed to get the opportunity to write the papers that would build his reputation in the academic world. He applied for various senior university roles and was never short-listed.

In his private life, the atmosphere at home was tense. His teenage children could be very difficult; he was always having painful conversations that sapped his energy. It was a couple of good friends and one of the professors who believed in him who helped James keep up his spirits. James's friends enabled him to keep going and ensure that he kept a positive demeanor. This professor helped James keep his work focused.

Eventually James got some key papers published and began to get one or two interviews. At last he was offered a post as a Reader in a neighboring university. James was for ever grateful to his two friends and the Professor, who had stuck with him and enabled him to work through the down moments. It was the resolve that he gained through the down moments that enabled him to take up a more senior post in the university and make a success of it.

What down moments have you been gripped by?

Nothing could lift John. His heart was in his boots; there was no joy in his face, his eyes were thousands of miles away, and his body was listless as he sat in the chair. Conversation with his family had gradually slowed to brief, staccato exchanges. One or two friends could help him break into a smile, but their patience had been sorely stretched. Would he stay like this for ever, or was there a chance that his old self would return? It looked as though it would be a long struggle. This might seem like a stark example, but many of us will have felt elements of being in the grip of down moments, unable to move on constructively.

Those who have never known down moments might have only scratched the reality of life, as it is the down moments that make us who we are. Without those times of emptiness we would not know the contrast with times of fulfillment. Sometimes we have to exist through down moments, however bleak they are.

Down moments can be trivial times when our pride has been slightly dented. We might have put a huge amount of effort into a particular event and no one seems to notice or care. Our pride is hurt and we grumble quietly to ourselves. They can be moments of regret when we do not live up to our or others' expectations of ourselves. There can be times when we feel let down by others.

Other down moments can be much more severe. A loved one dies, and the tail of grief goes on for many months. It can often take a couple of years to recover fully after a bereavement, with one down moment rapidly followed by another.

Our job prospects, once bright, might all of a sudden become less rosy. We are a rising star one day and a figure of the past the next. We have hitched our wagon to one leader, and then all of a sudden we lose our champion and we are isolated and on the periphery.

Some down moments seem to go on interminably. The relationship with a difficult teenager goes from bad to worse. Exchanges with the boss become increasingly difficult. Friendships, once joyful, become more and more strained. We seem to be caught in a spiral which goes from bad to worse. Nothing we do seems to stop the decline.

Sometimes down moments grip our whole being. We feel lost in an unending storm, racked by the elements and exhausted. At these times, strong, loyal friendships and caring, undemanding companionship can pull us through. The grip of depression can be cruel and devastating, but hanging on in there can lead to a new strength. We can end up with new insights into the paradox of frailty and fulfillment sitting alongside each other.

What types of down moment have gripped you? At the trivial end, it might be that your pride was hurt by the pain of an unfair comment denting your self-esteem. Sometimes down moments at work might have caused pain that seemed to go on for ever. On occasions you might be knocked sideways and become gripped by a feeling of rejection and find it very difficult to move on.

When have down moments had a positive outcome?

Henrietta talks of one month during her childhood when her mother passed away and her father decided to emigrate to the United States a couple of weeks later. She felt beaten up by the experience, but out of it came the resilience that enabled her to cope with many future reverses in both her family and her work life. The resilience that came from her childhood experiences gave her a persistence and resoluteness that enable her to cope with high-pressure work on various continents.

Harold talked of when his best friend was due to visit him and lost his life in a car crash on his journey to Harold's home. Harold was mortified: "Why did I suggest he come over for dinner?" He was full of anguish: "If I had just kept my mouth shut, my friend would not have died." Gradually, Harold accepted that it wasn't his fault and that a drunken driver had careered into his friend's car. Could any good come out of this tragic story? Harold, when he emerged from his grief, became a man of immense compassion. He could always see the risks that might flow from decisions. Sometimes this meant he became over-cautious, but often his kindly forewarning about potential consequences helped people to think through their true motives for a particular action.

We joke about mid-life crises, and yet a re-evaluation of what really matters to an individual in their 40s and 50s can have a profound effect on how they use the rest of their life. A mid-life crisis that undermines confidence can leave an individual a shadow of their former self, but mid-life reflection which starts with a sense of rejection and unhappiness can turn into a re-awakening and rejuvenation with a new flow of energy and creativity.

The disciple Peter knew highs and lows in his relationship with Jesus. He identified Jesus as the Son of God and as the Messiah, and more than most disciples he understood the impact of Jesus' teaching. On the other hand, Peter denied he knew Jesus three times when he followed him into the Temple Courts after Jesus had been taken prisoner by the Roman soldiers. After the cock crowed three times, Peter was mortified by his own denials. Yet out of this anguish came a disciple strengthened by his own display of weakness who was to become one of the first leaders of the Christian Church. Maybe he had to go through that time when he failed to acknowledge that he knew his own leader in order to build that resoluteness to lead the Christian Church.

Sometimes down moments are unavoidable

The woman in childbirth knows that whatever the pain, there is a purpose to the pangs of labor. The athlete who trains hard runs through the pain barrier to strengthen their physical resilience. The teenager who has to struggle with homework reaches the point at which the difficult subject matter has been mastered and they can move on to new and more interesting topics.

Sometimes there has to be a struggle or there is no outcome. The following story illustrates the simple truth that struggle is sometimes essential:

A man found the cocoon of an Emperor moth so that he could watch the moth emerge from the cocoon. One day a small opening appeared. The man watched for hours as the moth struggled to force its body through the little hole. Then it seemed to stop making any progress. It appeared as if it had got as far as it could and it could go no further. It seemed to be stuck. The man, in his kindness, decided to help the moth. He took a pair of scissors and snipped off the remaining bit of the cocoon so that the moth emerged easily. But it had a swollen body and small, shriveled wings. The man continued to watch the moth because he expected that at any moment the wings would enlarge and expand to be able to support the body, which would contract in time. But neither happened. The little moth spent the rest of its life crawling around with a swollen body and shriveled wings. It never was able to fly.

What the man in his kindness and haste did not understand was that the restricting cocoon, combined with the struggle required for the moth to get through the tiny opening, forced fluid from the body of the moth into its wings so that it would be ready for flight once it achieved its freedom. Freedom and flight could come only after the moth's struggle. By depriving the moth of its struggle the man interfered with this process of growth, with the result that the moth never attained its full beauty and mobility.

If moments of struggle can be a powerful influence for good, are there times when we allow tough moments to be an indulgence? We can sometimes wallow in our own misfortune. There is sometimes a risk that we share our sense of guilt or pain rather too generously and try to suck others into our own struggles. There can be an indulgent pleasure in focusing on the misfortunes of ourselves and others. Is there a danger that we define ourselves by our own down moments rather than our good moments? If we reflect on our down moments for too long, we become ever more pessimistic and unable to move into a better place.

Living with our down moments is part of self-awareness and of recognizing our own emotions. They provide the breadth and warmth of life. But distinguishing among different types of down moments is important – for example:

- The trivial down moments which are about status, pride and self-esteem
- The tough down moments of bereavement, relationship breakups and loss of work which cannot be dismissed lightly and might painfully toughen our character
- The tragic down moments which might knock our equilibrium and be very difficult to understand and move on from

What is inevitable is that we will each have our own mix of trivial, tough and tragic down moments. Perhaps regarding these moments as a gift to learn from seems too trite. But seeing them as part of the rich tapestry of life to be experienced and learned through can bring a healthy acceptance that down moments will happen.

Living with particular types of down moments

The rest of the chapter deals with specific examples of down moments.

When you lose authority

When things went wrong for Geraldine, she tended to close in on herself, come across as having lower energy and lose authority. She could make it difficult for herself by withdrawing so that her loss of authority seemed to become greater. Geraldine would turn the situation around by being relentless, tactically clever and willing to be opportunistic. Some people would underestimate Geraldine when she appeared to lose authority, but they underestimated her at their own peril. Geraldine had her own way of coping with loss of authority in meetings and with colleagues, and she knew that she would eventually turn a situation around through her resolve.

When you find it difficult to get fired up

Tom knew that he could sometimes get stuck in his comfort zone. He enjoyed working on particular activities but recognized after a while that this could mean a flatness in his manner. The danger was that the "Can I be bothered?" theme could affect some of his attitudes. It was sometimes difficult for him to get fired up. He could go onto automatic pilot without much adrenalin to keep him engaged in new approaches and ideas. The flatness did not necessarily lead to good reflective space.

Tom recognized this cycle. He knew that being too much in his comfort zone would sap his energy. He needed to create situations in which he was challenged both physically and intellectually. He needed there to be movement. A brisk walk could make all the difference. A challenging conversation would invariably help. He knew that he could get stuck feeling flat. He recognized that sometimes he did need to sit in his comfort zone in order to build some rest into his routine, but he knew that it was dangerous to allow this situation to go on for a long time.

When you receive negative feedback

When Richard heard negative feedback about the area for which he was responsible, and in which he had worked hard to ensure progress, he felt distinctly put out. But when he had calmed down he addressed the negative feedback by telling himself not to lose his rag. There was no valid reason to view the situation as hopeless. There was lots of evidence of progress, and he needed to hold his head up high. Yes, there were areas where change was needed, and action was in hand. But his affirmation to himself that the situation was not hopeless was important. Richard reiterated to himself that progress had been made and that there was an excellent platform for the future, while at the same time being utterly realistic about the need for practical improvement.

When you feel burdened

For Marion various issues she was dealing with felt like a burden. The weight seemed to get bigger and bigger, and the actions she took seemed not to have a huge impact. What helped Marion was talking through the issues in a factual way so that the practicalities were clear and the task did not grow into a huge mountain to climb. Chunking the task into pieces helped enormously and enabled progress to take place.

Building greater self-awareness about the reason for the darkness also helped. It was crucial for her not to become overly tired and get things out of proportion. Part of Marion's approach was to picture the burden as a heavy rucksack and gradually reduce the contents of the rucksack until it sat on her shoulders in a way with which she could cope.

When you have to live with your dark moods

Gillian was conscious that she went through dark moods that would grip her for hours at a time. She worked hard to understand what set these dark moods off and how best she could contain them. She did not aspire to remove the dark moods altogether, but she tried to diminish their effect. She began to laugh at them; she felt herself going through a dark tunnel and knew there would be light at the end. As soon as she began to see flickers of light she felt that she was moving on in a more positive way. For Gillian the crucial aspect was understanding the pattern and knowing that she would come out of the dark mood within a reasonable period.

When you need to overcome a major factual mistake

John talks of a major report that was due to be published the following day. Figures in the report had been checked regularly, but John thought it was worth one final check before the report was published. He read through the first few pages and noticed that a significant figure was badly wrong. It was potentially damaging, as this figure would inevitably be picked up by the media. Out of adversity was born a tremendous team spirit. The team spent half an hour working through what their next steps would be. A sequence of figures had to be redone; people worked into the night to ensure the figures were accurate, and a limited number of revised copies of the document were prepared so that the launch could go ahead as planned.

John was pleased in retrospect with his reaction. When he spotted the error his approach was not about recrimination but about ensuring that the document was revised correctly. There was such relief that the final product was accurate. New systems were put in place so that similar problems could not occur again. There were some wounded egos, but the fact that the team had worked so well to correct the error meant that the lessons learned were productive. John's over-riding emotion was gratitude that the error had been spotted rather than anger about why it had occurred in the first place.

When you feel stuck

Ben went through a period of feeling stuck. He felt out of touch with certain aspects of his work, and he would get to the end of the week exhausted. He did not feel he was making any significant progress in getting his staff to work together effectively. There was no capacity in the organization for thinking in new ways. Ben felt that his stuckness could become a downward spiral if he was not careful.

Ben's approach was to focus his time more effectively to ensure he was in touch with the areas of work which were most important for him. He had an away-day with the team to think hard about how they were going to work better together. He paced himself so that he did not end up exhausted on Friday evening. He put space in his diary to reflect about longer-term issues when the PC was safely turned off.

When you beat yourself up

Sylvia had a tendency to beat herself up. There were three stages:

1. Being in the moment and getting on with things
2. Feeling down when she allowed herself to reflect and see only limited progress
3. Allowing herself to believe that she had done the right thing when she began to see progress

For Sylvia there was always a danger of getting stuck in Stage 2. Her concern was to ensure that she moved from Stage 1 to Stage 3. Part of not getting stuck at Stage 2 was ensuring she got good feedback from those she trusted. It helped when she remembered the significant progress she had made on previous occasions. Recognizing her pattern and knowing whom to talk to were crucial in helping her move through the phase in which she normally beat herself up.

When you are digging a hole for yourself

Henry was conscious that he could sometimes get defensive and start digging a hole. When he got into particular down moments there was a real risk that he would make it worse by digging himself in. He knew that when this occurred, the right approach was to stop digging, stop regarding a particular issue as the be all and end all, move on to something else and shift his thinking to other parts of his life. It was about giving himself permission to accept that there would be ups and downs and recognizing it is OK to feel that things are not going well sometimes, but to stop making it worse by keeping digging.

When you are living with frustration

Yasif had a frustrating performance review with his boss. The boss had described him as a valuable, solid performer who had sorted out a lot of problems but had not made as much progress as necessary on big issues. Yasif felt frustrated by the lack of appreciation in his boss's comments and undervalued. He was suffering from dented pride.

For Yasif the best way of handling frustration was to acknowledge it, talk about it with one or two trusted others, be clear in his own mind about the progress that had been made, recognize the feeling of unfairness and then put in place some practical next steps.

When there is leakage from area of life to another

Brian was conscious that two bereavements in his family meant that he was not coming across as positive at work. His sadness showed. His colleagues were understanding, but after a while he recognized that the team was losing impetus because of his demeanor. He knew he had to compartmentalize his emotions so that they did not detrimentally affect his team. Trying to be cheerful at work was not straightforward, but he knew he had to try not only for his team but also for his own sense of moving on. Gradually he was able to be more cheerful and the team spirit lifted. At the same time he recognized that the grief would take two years to work itself through fully, so he was inevitably going to have to compartmentalize his emotions over an extended period.

Next steps

Down moments are always going to be with us. They can be some of the most formative moments in our lives. But how we handle them is crucial to our wellbeing. We need to be able to handle down moments in a way which builds up our capabilities rather than destroys them.

Questions to reflect on might be:

- Which are the down moments that have been most formative in my approach to life?
- Which pattern of down moments is most likely to affect me?
- What are the mechanisms that work best for me in coping with down moments effectively?
- What are some of the early warning signs I need to be conscious of so that I do not get stuck in down moments?
- How best can I share my experience of handling down moments in a way which will enable others to cope with their down moments effectively?

8 Crisis moments

Crisis moments can knock us off course, drain our energy and destroy our confidence. But sometimes crisis moments are the making of us; sometimes they enable us to develop new sources of resilience and demonstrate to us that we have reserves of inner strength that we were not fully aware of. Key tests are how we recover from crisis moments that have knocked us sideways and how we embed the learning from crisis moments in which we made more progress than we expected.

Roger's story

Roger was a doctor working in the Accident and Emergency department at a hospital. There were peaks and troughs in the work, but always within reasonable bounds. One day there was an explosion at a nearby factory, and many people were badly injured. A rush of injured people arrived at the hospital needing urgent attention.

The doctors and nurses became very focused. There was no sense of panic and no needless rushing around. There were no wasted words: instructions were clear and concise. There was a purposefulness and a clarity about priorities.

It was a crisis in one sense, with lots of people needing urgent attention. But there was no sense of crisis or panic in Roger and his colleagues. They knew what to do in a crisis. Instinctively, they made judgments about priorities and kept cool. They recognized when individuals in the team were getting over-tired and issued clear instructions for them to take a short break. On normal days there could be some bickering within the team, but as soon as there was an emergency they worked together smoothly and effectively. When the activity died down Roger and the team were able to relax and feel that they had handled the crisis well. The department had run like a well-oiled machine. Perhaps they even surprised themselves by how well they had worked together.

One person's crisis is another person's daily routine. Doctors, police and members of the armed forces are taught to deal with emergencies. It is part of their professionalism to be able to cope with the unexpected. For many of us, preparing for crises or the unexpected has not been part of our working experience.

What has been your learning from crisis moments?

Whether or not we have been prepared for crisis moments, they hit us. When we are caught by the unexpected we might freeze, go into overdrive, feel a sense of panic or want to pretend the crisis does not exist. Understanding our own human reaction to a crisis is central to handling it well.

Francis was driving down a narrow road when he was hit in the rear at a hidden intersection and his car careered off the side of the road into a stone pillar. His car was a write-off. He was shaken but did not feel injured. His first response was to get out of the car and phone his family to say, "I am alright, but the car is a write-off." He managed to keep calm, was apologetic to the other people involved, was relieved that there were no injuries and was happy to be physically checked over by a doctor. He became the safest driver in his family from them on. The car accident was a defining moment for Francis in terms of helping him recognize his own vulnerability and the need to be careful as a driver.

My father-in-law was part of the D-Day landings of the Allied Forces in Normandy in 1944. He was a doctor with the British forces but saw live action on a number of occasions. He was close to death three times, and years later he could picture coming face to face with a German soldier. Both of them moved away without a word. My father-in-law would treat Allied and German wounded soldiers with equal care. He handled crises with focus and thoughtfulness but did not want to spend time in later life talking about those experiences.

Benjamin was in a key role in deciding how to handle bomb alerts. If any bomb alert always led to the closure of the city's transportation system, then the economy would grind to a halt. But if every bomb threat was ignored, one day a bomb might go off, with drastic consequences. His team had developed clear guidelines about how to treat individual threats. They trusted the procedures and made judgments about when to take precautions and when to regard a call as a hoax. Benjamin had to live with the risk that they might make a wrong call; he had to handle potential crises on a regular basis but was able to keep his cool and not be rushed into hasty decisions.

Navigating through turbulent times

At Praesta Partners we talked to a range of leaders during 2008 about how best they navigated through turbulent times and coped with different types of crisis. The results of the action research were published in 2008 as *Riding the Rapids: How to Navigate through Turbulent Times*. This section summarizes some of the main conclusions from that research.

Many of the characteristics identified as important in dealing with turbulent times are leadership fundamentals. During such times strong leaders:

1. Maintain their core attitudes and beliefs, no matter how much pressure they come under
2. Tackle each new challenge clearly and calmly, leading from the front to inspire those around them
3. Know to look after themselves to maintain stamina and wellbeing for a lengthy and often exhausting period

Maintaining core attitudes and beliefs

Leaders talk of being under pressure to make uncomfortable decisions, being expected to find all the answers themselves and feeling overwhelmed by the enormity of their challenge. A common learning in turbulent times is that focusing on doing what you believe to be the right thing gives you a sense of personal integrity, self-worth and even accomplishment, no matter what the final outcome. What you regard as right can come from your own values and experiences or from having considered the perspective of trusted advisors.

We repeatedly hear about the immense effort required to keep doing what we believe is right when we are under pressure. It can be tempting to go for a quick win, make small compromises or focus on the most attractive numbers just to make others feel better or to make ourselves look good. By doing this we can inadvertently lose our way. The forces pulling at us can help clarify what we really believe. We sometimes truly discover what we believe is right only when we are pushed to make a difficult decision.

During challenging times it can be hard to admit that you cannot do something. It can feel like an admission of failure. However, one consistent message is that during turbulent times being honest with yourself is a considerable leadership strength. In particular this is about focusing your energy and time and recognizing when you might be about to lose it. Reaching for the impossible can lead to over-stretching to breaking-point. Success comes through knowing what things you do well and accepting the limits of your ability. It is also about recognizing what you, and you alone, can do and concentrating on this.

In turbulent times leaders talk of feeling disappointed, resentful, exhausted, angry or afraid. These are powerful emotions that fundamentally affect our ability to view things logically and to act rationally. The practical lesson is that if you feel yourself closing down, lacking confidence, blaming others or not listening, the right action is to acknowledge that you might be in danger of becoming emotionally overwhelmed. It is important to evaluate your impact and see how your reaction might be affecting your work and the people around you, and to step away and take a break from the situation, even for a short period.

Being positive means believing that no matter how intractable the challenge might appear, there is a way out of it. It is about focusing on what can be done, not what has gone wrong. Leaders emphasize the importance of grounded optimism rather than false optimism. Grounded optimism requires a constructive mindset combined with a healthy realism about what is going on.

Tackling each new challenge clearly and calmly

When faced with tackling decisions and issues during extreme turbulence, the most effective leaders continue to define their role, and their success, within the context of the bigger picture. They also have a sense of who they are and what they stand for, which goes beyond their current job. They therefore resist being consumed by any specific situation or crisis.

The results of our action research suggest that successful leaders do this by focusing on four things that make a difference: keeping a sense of perspective, setting priorities, having the right people around them and leading from the front.

Loss of perspective is one of the first things that leaders can experience during challenging, unpredictable times when they become unable to put each issue or decision in context and understand how real a threat it represents. Under pressure it is easy to feel drawn to action, and the normal thinking time can seem like a luxury. However counter-intuitive it might feel, it is critical to step back to think, even for a short time.

How do you put things into perspective while maintaining the necessary pace of decision-making during turbulent times? A past lesson for many has been the importance of having the best inputs possible and quick access to information to test your judgment and make focused decisions. You need to ensure you stay widely informed, even under pressure, to maintain perspective and keep your antennae tuned.

This might require searching more widely and deeply for opinions, data and ideas even if time is limited. When you gather information, it is critical to do so selectively and with a clear purpose to help you take action. This means avoiding the common pitfall of paralysis by analysis, where continual research becomes a substitute for decision-making and action. You cannot sit in your bunker and fall back on previous experience alone: it will not be enough.

Leaders stress the need to stay focused on four fundamental ways of informing decisions during turbulent times:

- *Get the best data and information you can.* You might have to work a bit harder for the right intelligence by challenging what you are told or spending the resources to get the best external help. During turbulent times people might tell you what you want to hear and put a gloss on things.
- *Listen to others' views.* You should actively seek opinions widely throughout your organization and beyond. It helps to discuss issues, get fresh thinking and listen to a broad range of people, not a narrow view. This means trying to remain open-minded and interested in opinions and to avoid shutting people down who might think you have already decided on the answers.
- *Have personal sounding boards.* Make sure you have trusted people to talk to and a safe space where you can speak your mind, say the unsayable, think the unthinkable and talk it through out loud. This will help get your mind straight. It will also ensure you are exploring the issues fully. Some of these people should come from outside the organization to give you a broad perspective. Often people find an executive coach helpful at this time.
- *Create personal space.* Regularly find places to think clearly on your own and gain inspiration, such as going for a long walk. The rest and space this creates can leave room for a breakthrough idea to come to you.

A leader ultimately has to make decisions and set direction for an organization. This is particularly difficult when the day-to-day reality is constantly changing and unpredictable. It is easy to get sucked into lurching from one crisis to another, to become a fire fighter. The most effective leaders during turbulence are as clear as possible with themselves and others about where they want to take their organization and what everyone needs to do to get there. At the same time they have the flexibility to adapt quickly when circumstances or perspectives change in the light of new information.

In terms of focusing the organization, leaders speak of the need to hold their nerve in the face of panic or pressure from others. This is about finding the courage to prioritize what will make the biggest difference to long-term success, and sometimes to choose among a set of equally unattractive options. These decisions might prove unpopular if they do not result in immediate action or results, but if you have invested in being informed, success comes through trusting your own judgment. Many leaders find that turbulent times open up opportunities to make radical change. Things that seemed impossible or unthinkable might now not only look feasible, but become necessary.

During times of extreme challenge, a leadership team needs to be high performing, with the right people in the right roles. The team needs to be loyal, committed, aligned and collaborative. A team can sometimes develop its most innovative ideas when it is put under pressure. Our action research suggested that during turbulent times it is crucial to be surrounded by people who are both on-side and able to disagree openly during debates before reaching agreement about what to do. It is the role of the leader to create an environment in which people feel encouraged to be honest and to question views and decisions when appropriate. It is not a place or a time for "yes" people or for dysfunction within a team.

If the pressure of uncertainty reveals flaws or gaps in experience in a team, leaders need to make the necessary changes and to make them quickly. There is not the luxury of time to wait and see. Quick action can be painful, but it is essential. Pulling together under real pressure can result in amazing creativity of output. Pressure on the group to think the unthinkable can engender creativity and ideas of a level previously not seen.

During times of uncertainty, stress and panic, people need to see a leader who is calm, focused and inspiring. You cannot be like this from behind a closed door. This is a time for visible, personal leadership of your people, for keeping everyone informed and for publicly setting the tone for how you expect your whole organization to react and behave. During extreme uncertainty, it is unlikely you will have many answers for people's questions. However, the experience of many leaders has shown the dangers of going silent with people in the organization and spending too much time in a huddle with your immediate team. Silence breeds rumor and negative energy.

People need information to understand where to focus, how to prioritize and when to offer ideas. It is vital to communicate constantly and to keep the dialogue open. In turbulent times it is important to keep talking, not only in meetings but when walking around the organization. If there is no clear answer you can always explain your direction, what you are focusing on to solve your problems and what you want people to be working on now to keep things on course.

As a leader it is important to be conscious that everything about you gives a message to your organization: not only your words, but your posture, facial expression, tone of voice and appearance. People will look for any signals that you feel things are out of control. The perception of your mood will spread like wildfire and will often become distorted through gossip. When a CEO asked his Chairman what was the single most important thing he should be doing, the reply was "Smile." The Chairman then referred to the cheerleader aspect of a leader's role in turbulent times, which might require putting on a leadership mask. This can be extremely difficult when your working environment is visible to others, which makes finding safe personal space during the day all the more critical.

Looking after yourself to maintain stamina and wellbeing

Leading an organization, its people and yourself through radical changes and pressures requires a high level of stamina and personal strength. To many leaders, focusing on their own wellbeing can feel like self-indulgence. It can feel as if every moment matters and that it is important to dig in, to work all the hours you can to ensure that the organization and its people are on track. This approach might work in a short-term crisis. The danger is that if you don't look after yourself over the longer term, you can lose perspective and start to lack the energy to make tough decisions. This can be exacerbated by the fact that, under pressure, many people find it difficult to sleep and so suffer the adverse effects of sleep deprivation.

There is growing evidence that looking after yourself fundamentally affects your effectiveness and ability to be at your best as a leader. It is not an optional extra; it is the foundation for your leadership success. Being in good shape will mean that you have the inner resources to dig deep into your energy reserves and the resilience not to let the tank run dry.

The evidence from our action research at Praesta Partners points to four areas of wellbeing that are well worth keeping a focus on. Each gives a personal 'hinterland' of interests and perspective that allow you to succeed. You should assess which areas are most important to you and how you can ensure they remain a part of your life even during the busiest times;

■ *Physical wellbeing*. Building stamina through a combination of personal fitness and relaxation time which renews creative and mental energy.

- *Emotional wellbeing.* Finding a state of equilibrium helps you to remain calm. For some people this balance is supported by their relationships; for others, by their sense of self-worth and unique value.
- *Intellectual wellbeing.* Engaging your mind in something different from everyday work, no matter how trivial, can be a source of relief and can stimulate creativity.
- *Spiritual wellbeing.* Knowing what matters most in your life keeps things in perspective, whether this knowledge comes from enduring interests or relationships or is rooted in belief and faith.

The overall conclusion from our work with leaders navigating through turbulent times was that their experience of learning to live with a higher level of challenge, pressure and stress was a normal part of working life rather than a short-term crisis. They require resilience, stamina and focus. Resilient leaders – those who are physically and mentally strong – are able to accept change, to learn from it and to thrive under pressure. They regard challenges as an opportunity, as a chance to learn and to deepen their experience. Their ability to be flexible, positive and energetic comes to the fore and separates them from other leaders.

The booklet Jane Stephens and I wrote on this subject has been received very positively. Some individuals have talked about it enabling them to be determined to take back control of their lives, with the result that they have emerged from turbulence stronger and wiser.

Essential leadership characteristics in hard times

Ram Charan, in his book *Leadership in the Era of Economic Uncertainty*, echoes a number of these themes. He sets out six essential leadership traits for hard times:

- *Honesty and credibility.* Your authority derives not from omniscience but from your ability to facilitate understanding and solutions. Level with people; tell them how you see the world, acknowledge the limits of your understanding and ask them for their own views.
- *The ability to inspire.* Many people do not see what will turn things around; many are close to losing hope. Work with your team to toughen their resolve to get through the storm successfully. Help them develop one or two realistically optimistic pictures of what can lie ahead.

- *Real-time connection with reality.* Keep updating your picture of reality, continuously monitoring change and impending change through ground-level intelligence. Put all of your concrete external information on the table, however bad it might be. Don't get locked into one view of things.
- *Realism tempered with optimism.* Focus your people on the vision of what is possible and energize them to search for the actions that will realize that vision. This is where leadership becomes a performance art, introducing that touch of optimism that taps psychological reserves to deal with bad news and transform fear into action.
- *Managing with intensity.* You must dig into the right detail with much higher frequency than ever before. You have to be interactive – listening as well as explaining, answering questions, taking the conversation to the next level and then doing it again and again.
- *Boldness in building for the future.* Resist the pressure to short-change the future. It will take imagination and guts to place strategic bets with no guaranteed payout when there is little money available.

Allowing yourself to be shaped by the way you handle a crisis

David Bell, the Permanent Secretary at the Department for Education, recalls needing to handle a crisis as soon as he arrived in the department. He talks of there being a moment for any leader in any organization when they are tested under fire. For him this moment was 10 days into the job. It was high stakes, with his credibility at stake. He got through it, and the result was a very good relationship with the Secretary of State. He showed that he could handle a crisis. The experience defined for him how you should behave in a crisis. The shadow you cast as a leader is crucial during a crisis. The physical act of slowing down is important. You set the tone. People can look ragged in a crisis; your personal demeanor is important. It is important to demonstrate that you are above the fray. In the heat of battle you have to stand back.

David acknowledged that during the crisis he made a particular mistake. He said to the Secretary of State privately afterward that it was his mistake not to have cleared with her in advance a conversation with an external party. Admitting the mistake was an important moment, and it helped David build an excellent relationship with the Secretary of State. In crises, mistakes do happen. David's perspective was that it is important to acknowledge the mistake immediately. If you don't admit it to others, there will be a nagging doubt about your judgment or your trustworthiness.

The over-riding message from so many leaders dealing with crises is the importance of remaining calm. Those who were heavily involved in the economic crisis of late 2008 talk about the experience being both exhilarating and exhausting. The lessons have been about the value of keeping your composure, looking in control, delegating effectively and maintaining an aura of calmness.

What leaders often observe is that during a crisis some people rise up into the leadership space and others hide away. One key attribute of any leader is the ability to spot those people who are rising into the space and to enable them to be effective leaders. This also means being conscious of who begins to disappear and to become less effective. It might be necessary to encourage and re-stimulate these people or to ease them out into a role that they can cope with better.

Next steps

Crisis moments can shape us or break us. Building resilience so that we can cope well in a crisis and lead others effectively is precious. Keeping calm in a crisis, maintaining core attitudes and beliefs, and knowing how to look after ourselves are central to success.

Questions to reflect on might be:

■ What have I learned from those who have handled crises well?
■ When have I handled a crisis well, and what did I learn about myself?
■ How am I building my resilience to be able to cope with a future crisis effectively?
■ How can I best keep calm in a crisis?
■ What might be the next crisis that I need to address?

9 Moments of anger

Moments of anger can be creative or destructive. Sometimes, when we are moved by moments of righteous anger, we crystallize our views on a particular issue and become more purposeful. On other occasions, when our anger is indignation, it can be disruptive to ourselves and others and can take a long time to rebuild. Handling moments of anger well is about observing yourself, dealing with irritation, managing resentment and being conscious of how you respond when people let you down.

John's story

John had got angry once too often. John held a senior position and had a key relationship with a major stakeholder organization. At one critical meeting he lost his cool completely; it looked almost as if he might hit his opposite number. He appeared to be out of control; it was destructive anger at its worst. It looked as if a relationship which had taken such a long time to build up would be destroyed for ever.

Following the wise counsel of others, he calmed down. He needed very little encouragement to accept that he needed to go and see the person with whom he had been angry and offer a full apology. This individual was initially surprised but then responded by saying that he recognized that he had been part of the cause of the angry outburst. They shook hands on a new relationship. The anger had been dissipated, and both of them were seeing the future in a different light. In their subsequent meetings, initially there was a hint of suspicion about whether the anger would recur, but once that hesitation was seen to be unfounded, the working relationship became all the stronger. The quality of the working relationship was now even better than before because the angry outburst had been cathartic and enabled the relationship to be redefined on a much more secure basis. On this occasion the moment of anger led to a positive improvement because of an honest expression of regret, remorse and reconciliation.

I could sense that I was in danger of a moment of anger. We were due to walk sections of the pilgrimage route to Santiago de Compostela. The tour company literature was based on an early evening departure, which meant I could do a day's work first. But the flight time had now been switched to the morning, which was going to disrupt my plans. Alternative flight arrangements were going to be complicated and costly. I had a difficult conversation with a customer services representative. When I began to feel a sense of anger, I knew it was time to withdraw from the conversation.

What have been your angry moments?

Angry moments come in a great variety of shapes and sizes. Every commuter into a big city has had the experience of delayed trains, or the absence of any information about the reasons for the delay, and knows the personal aggravation that this can cause. The train carriage squashed with grumpy commuters after a sequence of train cancellations can be full of pent-up anger evidenced by the abrupt turning of pages of newspapers or by irritated phone conversations.

Ron plans his diary meticulously, with appointments at regular intervals. When someone is late the whole sequence is disrupted. If an individual cancels at short notice Ron feels cross that his time is being wasted. Anger gets in the way of using the available time constructively. Ron knows that the disruption of his diary has spoiled his equilibrium. Sometimes he handles it well and recognizes that the gap in his diary is an opportunity. But often there is hurt pride that someone, by canceling, has stood him up.

George is focused in his work, but sometimes he can lose his cool and utter loud expletives. He never does this in front of other people and would be mortified if people ever heard him. What sets off his anger are e-mails from people who aren't listening or have missed the point or are being completely unrealistic. He knows that an angry e-mail back will make the situation worse. Anger comes out in the privacy of his own room, with the result that once he has dissipated his emotions he is able to respond rationally and persuasively. He reflects on whether this type of anger is useful in getting him into a better frame of mind or whether it is destructive. It is an aspect of his personality which he knows he is going to have to wrestle with.

Helen was angry about the way she had been treated at work. She had given much more time and energy to her job than had been required. She had become indispensable and was the glue that ensured a whole sequence of projects held together well. A promotion opportunity came up elsewhere in the organization. She put lots of energy into her application and her presentation, but she came second. There were nice words about how well she had done and about her opportunities for the long term. She sensed she had become so indispensable where she was that her bosses were reluctant to see her promoted into this other role. A hint of anger was aggravated by her awareness of the limited experience of the successful candidate and by all the hard work she had put into making a success of her job.

Do you empathize with any of these stories when a moment of anger wells up inside you? Are you conscious that anger can be destabilizing?

Handling anger well

What works for you in terms of reducing the destabilizing effects of moments of anger? Maybe controlling moments of anger involves:

- Being conscious of the destructive effect that anger can have on relationships and the time it takes to rebuild them
- Walking away from a situation in which you begin to feel angry and trying to see that situation in a wider context
- Holding your tongue and counting to 10
- Turning to another activity which is very different in its content and approach

When we feel anger about a particular issue it is unlikely that we can remove that anger at a stroke. We might have gradually to tame the anger and focus the energy it generates rather than pretend that it is not there. Running, cycling, walking briskly, swimming and even cutting the grass are all palliatives that many people find work well. Understanding our trigger points and the palliatives that work for us can provide a self-awareness that is important for our wellbeing. It can be worth writing down:

- Which issues am I most likely to get angry about?
- What are the trigger points that can set off my anger?
- How do I know that I am at risk of getting angry? For example, do I feel certain physical sensations that alert me to this possibility?
- What are the most effective means for me of stopping the sense of anger becoming destructive?

Some people find the advice not to let the sun go down while you are still angry to be helpful.

Can anger ever be good?

Sometimes unfairness or injustice needs a firm response. Righteous indignation can help draw clear boundaries and inform next steps. Sometimes righteous indignation can be an indulgence that leads to aggression and self-indulgence. It should always be tested against wider values and the perceptions of trusted others.

If there were no anger about unfairness in society or the abuse of different groups of people or the misuse of the physical environment or the destructive power of drugs or alcohol, then we would be drifting into selfish hedonism. Thoughtful, controlled anger can lead to change which improves the lot of those currently disadvantaged in one way or another.

You might feel angry about the unruly behavior of young people in your town or city at night. Being angry doesn't help, whereas talking to young people, helping to run a sports club, offering to mentor at the local school or donating funds to organizations working with young people can have a profound effect. The key question is, How do we turn our anger about what we see happening around us into a set of constructive actions?

When Jesus overturned the tables of the money-lenders in the Temple, was this a thoughtless, provocative act or a clear statement reminding people why the Temple was there and how it should be regarded? It was provocative, but it was not pointless. It sent a clear message that the Temple was to be a house of prayer and not a den of thieves. As a result, the religious authorities knew Jesus meant business. He was not only a good teacher; he was prepared to take action that some would regard as destructive in order to make a point. The anger of Jesus in the Temple was focused and explained. It was not random or irrational.

Sometimes dealing with angry moments is about establishing a positive dream for the future. In his "I have a dream" speech, delivered to a civil rights march in Washington, DC, in 1963, Martin Luther King Junior turned anger into a dream. He talked of not wallowing in the valley of despair. He talked of a dream that one day on the Red Hills of Georgia the sons of former slaves and the sons of former slave owners would be able to sit down together at a table of "brotherhood." He said, "I have a dream that my four little children will one day live in a nation where they will not be judged by the color of their skin but by the content of their character."

Martin Luther King turned anger into a constructive dream for the future. Thirty years later Nelson Mandela was holding out a dream in

South Africa. He had turned anger into the need for forgiveness and reconciliation. The speech he gave on the evening of his election victory in 1994 was full of generosity not anger. He talked of holding out a hand of friendship to the leaders of all parties and their members, and asking all of them to work together to tackle the problems faced by a nation. He said, "Now is the time for celebrations, for South Africans to join together to celebrate the birth of democracy. ... Let us build the future together and toast a better life for all South Africans."

Questions to ask ourselves about turning our righteous indignation to good effect might be:

■ What unfairness in the world makes me cross, and what am I prepared to do about it?
■ What unfairness in the workplace makes me cross, and what am I prepared to do about it?
■ What forms of waste of material or human resources makes me cross, and what am I prepared to do about it?

The opposite of anger can be indifference. Sometimes if we suppress moments of anger too much we can create the lethargy of indifference. Elie Wiesel was an inmate at Auschwitz. In a speech to the US Congress in April 1999 he talked of indifference as being tempted to look away from victims and finding it troublesome to be involved in another person's pain and despair. He described indifference as more dangerous than anger or hatred. He wrote, "Anger can at times be creative. One writes a great poem, a great symphony, one does something special for the sake of humanity because one is angry at the injustice that one witnesses, but indifference is never creative. ... Indifference elicits no response. Indifference is not a response. Indifference is not a beginning; it is an end." He went on to describe indifference as always being the friend of the enemy as it benefits the aggressor – never the victim, whose pain is magnified whenever he or she is forgotten.

We might struggle with our moments of anger, but perhaps it is more important to struggle with our moments of indifference. How do we best view pain or unfairness in the world or in the workplace so that we avoid the trap of indifference but also ensure we are focused in what we think and do?

Are there moments of indifference that perhaps ought to be moments of anger? Questions to ask ourselves might be:

■ What am I indifferent to where perhaps I ought to respond more critically?

- How do I currently indulge my indifference?
- In what two areas might I change my attitude of indifference into action?

It is not realistic to expect to turn indifference into action in every area of our lives. The result would be exhaustion and a dissipation of energy. Realism necessitates that we will appear indifferent to some instances of unfairness. The test is whether we have chosen wisely in deciding where to focus our energy.

Maybe it is through a combination of being willing to dream dreams, believing that reconciliation is possible and being conscious when our indifference is blinding us that we can move on and turn indifference into constructive action in specific areas.

Practical examples of dealing with moments of anger

The following are examples of how individuals have dealt effectively with different types of moments of anger.

When people let you down

Pauline is a Managing Director in a big transport organization. She says that when she begins to feel angry she can feel red mist rising up. Her approach in meetings is not to hide the anger but to put it on the table. She recalls one occasion when she thought she had reached an agreement with someone in her team prior to a negotiation. Within a couple of minutes, this team member appeared to join the other side. She was furious with him and let that show. He later acknowledged that he had been wrong but suggested that it would have been better if her anger had been shown in private rather than with other members of the team present.

For Pauline it is important that people understand the depth of feeling and the implications when they have caused anger in others. She also recognizes that managing feelings is important: anger can be a tool, but she no longer uses it in the heat of the red mist.

When resentment needs to be handled carefully

When Simon's reporting line was shifted from one boss to another he felt short-changed. He had a sense of the rug being pulled from under his feet. He was resentful because he had played no part in making the decision. Dealing with the resentment was not easy, but he found ways of coping and eventually found himself on a new job he would never have had if he'd stayed in the original reporting line. There were lessons for him about how quickly things can change. What helped him cope were his inner resources, working with a coach, recognizing that he needed to handle his resentment well and acknowledging that similar transitions he had been through before had worked out for the best.

When you are observing yourself and your own reactions

When Beatrice applied for a big Chief Executive role, she worked hard and prepared thoroughly. But the interview was disastrous; she went on and on. The feedback was that she had been undisciplined, and the consequence was that she felt bruised. The defining moment was the advice that less is more. At the next interview she was very disciplined and was successful. After feeling bruised at the end of the first interview and conscious of her own reaction she had sought wise counsel, which she immediately implemented, with the desired outcome of success in the second interview.

For Beatrice observing herself is important. She has the self-awareness to know that she will probably be quite tetchy today. She knows that what derails her is not getting enough sleep. For Beatrice, observing and understanding herself is important in dealing with tetchiness effectively.

When dealing with irritation

Marcus talks about the most difficult down moments as moments of irritation. He talks about irritation sweeping over him which can mean that his time is not used at all effectively. For Marcus the answer is understanding the causes of irritation and the early warning signals, and using tried-and-tested approaches to minimize and dissipate irritation or channel it in constructive ways.

When watching the consequences of anger is important

John, a University Registrar, tells a delightful story about signage at a university. He was frustrated by the number of signs around the university that were out of date. He gave a message that these signs were to be removed. He was then told that behind one of the signs that had been removed was an old sign referring to the university of which the current university had once been part. This was exactly the outcome that John did not want. The boss had said that the sign should be removed; this was done, but it revealed a greater problem which the person removing the sign had not appreciated.

A key reflection for John was, whatever action you take, watch the consequences and then, when you are tempted to anger, do try to see the funny side of the situation.

When watching your posture can help

Hazel could easily feel derailed in some situations and become intense and angry. Some of the practical approaches she took when going to potentially emotionally charged meetings were arriving composed and in good time, being effectively prepared, being clear in her own mind how she was going to approach a conversation, going in with a positive view of the other participants and, critically, sitting in a comfortable posture which enabled her to be composed and authoritative. She knew that as soon as she began to look tetchy, the conversation would be less productive. Holding her posture right was for her the best means of keeping her equilibrium as she wanted it to be.

When not to smile

Leonora was conscious that if she became nervous she would smile. The smile was a powerful tool at her disposal for building relationships and reaching agreement about next steps, but on occasions her smile could get in the way and give people the impression that she was content with an outcome when in reality she was deeply unhappy. If she was nervous or uncertain, the default smile could put people entirely on the wrong track. Leonora trained herself to be careful not to give false signals by smiling at the wrong time.

When holding the moment is important if there is a risk of going out of control

Hilary talks about being bad at savoring a moment and holding onto it. He recognizes the risk of rushing through moments and getting ever more emotionally involved in situations. He talks about needing to know the moments when he is likely to move from being emotionally in control to being emotionally out of control. He talks about the importance of creating stillness so that when he begins to feel strongly about something, he can keep hold of his emotions. He recognizes that as soon as he begins to feel out of control emotionally it can lead to damaging and unforeseen consequences.

Next steps

We have reflected on different sorts of moments of anger and their implications. We have seen anger as a force for good and ill. Understanding your anger and where it is coming from and knowing how to deal with it are perhaps among the most important skills of leadership. Next steps might be increasing your self-awareness about anger, including when it can be destructive and when it can be a focus of your energy and make a positive difference.

Key points to reflect on might be:

■ When is anger destructive for me, and how best can I control that anger?

■ How can I best reduce the likelihood of being gripped by destructive anger?

■ When can a sense of anger or injustice in me be a power for good?

■ In what ways do I want to avoid indifference and use a sense of controlled anger to make a constructive difference?

■ How best can I move on so that anger is turned into constructive thoughts and actions?

SECTION E

Treasuring the moment

This section is about treasuring the moment. Often we rush on from key moments and do not enjoy them enough or get the most out of them.

The section looks in turn at:

- Making each moment matter
- Accepting the truth of hard messages
- Embedding learning moments

Moments we treasure might be positive moments which have been joyful and engaging. Moments we treasure can also be times when we have learned hard truths and have appreciated the value of clear feedback. Sometimes moments we treasure are when we have learned something important about ourselves or the context in which we operate. That learning has altered our perspective in a profound and sometimes life-changing way.

It is not an indulgence to take pleasure in moments that are important to us. Treasuring good times and moments provides a bank of stories or a set of illustrations that can keep us going when life feels tougher.

10 Making each moment matter

Sometimes moments just pass us by. We can fail to realize the significance of certain moments. Sometimes we can enjoy good moments even more and not feel it is an indulgence to do so. Making each moment matter can mean living in the moment, photographing the moment, celebrating the moment and turning difficult moments into a positive step forward for the future. Making each moment matter is about not rushing continually; it can be about slowing down and creating shafts of stillness and allowing yourself to smile.

William's story

William had always been ambitious. He was determined to make a success of his working life. He would rush from one activity to another without a moment's hesitation. He was determined to make each moment matter.

But for some people he was so frenetic he made them edgy and they did not use their time well as a consequence. As time went on William became ever more driven and ambitious. Some enjoyed his hyperactivity; others found it increasingly difficult and irritating.

A good colleague took him out for a drink and gave him clear messages about slowing down. If he wanted to make each moment matter he needed to use his time differently. He needed to stop burdening people with his expectations and allow them space to breathe. Gradually William began to pace himself better and set different criteria for making each moment matter. He became less his own judge of the importance of a particular moment; he relied much more on whether his staff or the people he was working with felt that their time together was valuable. William recognized that he had to go slow to go fast.

At the start of each year I send a one-page note out to my coaching clients and contacts. At the start of a recent year I reflected on which moments are likely to matter most to people in their leadership roles and sent out the following note.

What is success this coming year?

How best do you approach a year which is bound to involve major change? How do you keep a positive attitude when there are major uncertainties? What are the fixed points about your approach which will help ensure you keep the events of the year in perspective?

Three elements might be to be candid, composed and clear. Under these three themes good questions to ask yourself might be:

Candid: How do I remain utterly objective and unbiased?
             How willing am I to speak the truth when others are being pushed along with the tide?

Composed: How best can I keep a cool head when the pressure is on?
             How can I bring a wider perspective when others are lost in the detail?

Clear: How do I ensure that I am using my time and energy well? Am I confident where I can add most value?

A successful year might involve:

- *Creating shafts of stillness* so that whatever the pace there are moments each day when you can breathe, clear your brain and put the events of the day in a wider context
- *Enabling quality conversations* so that there is always dialogue which encourages, stretches and challenges your thinking and action and those of the people you work with
- *Allowing yourself to smile* so that whatever is thrown at you there are moments when you see the funny side and share humor with colleagues, friends and family

Might a few moments reflecting on the thoughts above help position you for the New Year and all it holds? Success is not just about what we deliver this next year but about our wellbeing, our capacity to encourage and enable others, and our ability to keep a clear perspective about what is most important.

What I was trying to do in this message was strike a balance between activity and reflection. The activity is about being candid, composed and clear. Reflection is about creating shafts of stillness, enabling quality conversations and allowing yourself to smile. Making each moment matter depends on the right balance between activity and reflection. The balance will vary depending on the situation and our personality, but we need reflection to inform our action, and action to turn a reflection into purposeful outcomes.

Be absorbed in the moment

For many of us there is a risk of always thinking about something else and not living in the present moment. We want to be purposeful and always thinking about the future, but the consequence might well be that we do not use the present to best effect. We are cautious about not wanting to abandon ourselves to the current moment.

Clive is the Finance Director of a large organization. For many years the closest he came to being fully absorbed in the moment was when he played bridge. The pleasurable anticipation of a known event was a powerful attraction. But when he played the game of bridge he would hear the music slightly differently on each occasion.

It is worth reflecting on which activities completely absorb us and whether they refresh us. Complete preoccupation with a limited range of activities can make us dull and selfish. But celebrating our engagement in specific activities that completely absorb us can provide an escape from painful reality and recharge our batteries and our sense of purpose.

Key questions might be:

- What activities completely absorb me?
- What was the impact on me of a time when I was completely absorbed in an activity?
- Which other activities might I become completed absorbed in, in a way which will be constructive or enable me to relax?

Many parents speak of the importance of living in the moment. Parents in leadership positions often remember their time at home with young children as formative. It might well have taught them to enjoy standing at a bus stop and just be there thinking about nothing. Being with young children means that you want to concentrate on being in the moment. There can be important parallels in the working world.

Sometimes you just have to wait. These are bus stop moments. You have a nice, structured, productive and ambitious life and then you have a baby. The baby controls you and not you the baby. You cannot predict how the baby is going to control you. Ellen talked of always having two plans when she was with her baby, namely, if the baby is asleep I will do X; if the baby will not go to sleep I will go to see the ducks.

Ellen often applies this two-plan technique in her work. Under Plan A you can do specific things, but when you cannot control the moment it is time for Plan B and you just have to do what needs to be done. But for Ellen it is not just a choice between a pre-prepared plan and going with what needs to be done in the moment; it is also about envisaging a Plan C, which is flexing what needs to be done and always being willing to adapt while still ensuring that some of the plan you want to carry out gets done.

Capture the moment

In my 20s I rarely carried a camera. I thought it was enough to capture pictures in my memory. But the arrival of our first child brought a completely different approach, with photographing each stage of our children's development taking on a special significance. This was about capturing the moment with relentless regularity. When each of our children reached the age of 18 we gave them a photograph album which depicted the first 18 years of their lives. This was a joyful photographic memory compiled as much for the benefit of the parents as for the youngster.

Each picture told a story, and again and again the albums have been shown to friends, with the stories leading to lots of laughter. On some of our walls at home, we have collages of photographs from different years which act as a permanent reminder of many good memories.

It might seem trite to talk about photographic memories, but photographs on our desk or in an album can slow us down and remind us of the moments that are most important to us. If they bring joy back into our thoughts they have done their job well. My screensaver in my office for a number of years was a photograph of my older son and a friend at the road sign welcoming them to England after they had cycled from John O'Groats to Gretna Green: the screensaver made me smile whatever mood I was in.

Watch an expert use each moment well

Whatever our area of work, we often undervalue our own skills. Observing a specialist at work can be uplifting and enable us to reflect on our own skills.

I recently observed a cork farmer harvest cork. The farmer hits the bark of the cork tree with just the right intensity. The sharp, light axe cuts into the bark and through the cork but does not damage the tree. Using the back of the axe, the farmer taps the cork bark to loosen it and pushes the wedge-shaped handle of the axe into the vertical incision to lever off the cork bark. Within a minute the cork farmer has stripped the bottom 8 feet of a tree. The thickness of the cork is a pretty regular 35 mm. The top-quality material is made into corks for wine bottles, the medium-quality cork is used for disks, washers and shoe soles, and the rest is ground up to make granules, which are processed to form sheeting, tiles and insulating material.

Watching the cork farmer at work, I saw the delicate balance in the precision of his cutting and the harvesting of the precious cork. The removal of the protective cork produces a severe crisis in the life of the tree, but it does not kill it because the cork is composed of cells which are already dead. Beneath the cork is the cambium, which is very much alive and carries the sap to the upper part of the tree.

It is usually possible to de-cork the trees only between mid-June and mid-August, as during this hot period the volume of sap in the cambium increases and the damp layer which forms between the living cambium and the dead cork makes it possible to separate the two. Prizing off the cork before its time would damage the underlying cambium, spoiling future de-corking and possibly shortening the productive life of the tree.

The joy is watching the cork farmer operating precisely and quickly without damaging the tree. Can you think of specialists you have watched whose skill you have been impressed by, be they athletes, tennis players, carpenters, engineers, artists or musicians? Celebrating their skills can give us space and enable us to reflect on and celebrate the skills that we bring.

Accept painful memories

In a talk I gave at a carol service I invited people to look at a flickering candle and suggested that it was both moving and still at the same time. It was both small and bright. It was both incidental and poignant. I encouraged people to think about the flickering memories of Christmases past, which can be like an old black-and-white movie where one frame merges into another in the same way as pictures of Christmases past flicker across our memories. It might be remembering the presents we opened or our children opened or our children's children opened. It might be singing carols in churches or on street corners which are now geographically far away.

I encouraged reflection on flickering memories of Christmases past which were both joyful and sad: joyful memories of fun and affectionate memories of loved ones no longer physically alive. I suggested that flickering memories of Christmases past are to be accepted, enjoyed and acknowledged. They have helped form us as we are, whether we like it or not. My theme was accepting the flickering memories of Christmases past as part of what we bring to the future. Perhaps as we look at a flickering candle it calms us enough to be able to focus on the significance of our memories and what Christmas is really about.

Christmas can often be a time of painful memories, when we recall loved ones no longer with us and opportunities we once had that are long gone. But painful memories can be a springboard for our own resolve for the future. Painful memories of loved ones can bring us back to the values that they stood for and the significance of those values for us today.

In that talk at the carol service I encouraged people to reflect on what, like the candle, flickered for them. What might be their flickering hopes and dreams for the future? Maybe the candle flame in them is a flicker of interest or concern or compassion or passion or aspiration or joy. When an individual consciously moves on from memories past into the future, there is a desire to make a difference in new ways, a wish to encourage others more and to move on with joy not resentment. Sometimes a flicker needs a gentle breeze of encouragement, a sheltered environment which does not snuff it out, and time to grow in strength. My message at that carol service was that in the pace of the present and the pleasure or pain of the past, we should not forget what is flickering about the future.

Review how you have made moments matter

Periodic stock-takes can provide refreshing insights into which moments have been most important. Some of these moments might have passed us by, but they might have been the occasion when we began to view an individual more positively or to add a particular approach to our repertoire, or when we began to believe that we could be effective in chairing meetings. Such moments can be far more life-changing than we realize at the time.

As Ben and I reviewed the past three months, he talked about:

■ Positive external assessments of the work he had been doing
■ Taking opportunities to be more assertive
■ Building up more external experience to add to his CV
■ Representing his organization more often at external meetings

- Lots of examples of his being more decisive
- Clear interventions on subjects such as future strategy

After reviewing each strand we looked at the overall development. Ben concluded:

- There had been a lot of good progress.
- His assertiveness had become stronger
- He was understanding himself more and planning in advance which part of his repertoire he was going to use in a particular context.

We celebrated the recognition he had received from a number of people. I encouraged him to accept the value of that recognition. For the future, we talked about keeping up his energy levels through doing new things and being clear about the business benefits of each of his activities. In terms of continuing to grow his assertiveness, we talked about being clear on the answers to two questions:

- What do I most need to do today?
- What do I not need to do today?

Jim had been through a difficult period but had now moved to a new job and was making progress. He summarized the positive things that were happening:

- I am beginning to get the team established in the way I want.
- I am building a good relationship with my boss.
- I am getting home earlier and feel less tired.
- I am going to the gym more often and sleeping better.
- The job is exciting and interesting, and my home life is more fulfilling too.

Taking stock of his progress enabled Jim to be clear about which moments mattered most to him. He concluded that what mattered most was:

- Working a disciplined day, starting early but not leaving too late
- Leaving work at work and using more physical exercise as a means of de-cluttering his mind from work
- Feeling confident that he had moved on from previous difficult experiences, was now appreciated at work and was making a good contribution in his new role

Taking stock might seem indulgent, but it is as we take stock that we crystallize what we have learned and can appreciate the moments that have made the biggest difference.

Turn problems into opportunities

Making each moment count is about taking opportunities to turn problems into something different. Maureen tells a story about an away-day for her directorate. A cleaner came into the room toward the end of the day, and the facilitator made a rather unfortunate dismissive remark. Maureen knew that she had to redeem the situation and ensure that the participants left the meeting on a positive note. She asked everyone to do some of the clearing of the room so that there was less work for the cleaner to do. This went down well. For Maureen it was about being opportunistic and turning a difficult situation to advantage. It was about bringing a sense of good cheer at the end of the meeting and not letting it end on a sour note.

Next steps

We have looked at the significance of different sorts of moments that matter. I encourage you to treasure those moments and their significance for you. Often this will be about good moments, but sometimes it will be about painful or difficult moments out of which strength of character or new opportunities have been born.

Questions to reflect on might be:

- When do I live in the moment in an uncluttered way?
- How could I use photographs to reinforce moments that matter?
- Can I take stock periodically in a way that crystallizes good moments?
- Can I draw the good out of painful moments?
- Can I build in enough reflection to complement the action so that I enjoy a mixture of different sorts of moments?

11 Accepting the truth of hard messages

Hard messages are often difficult to take. If we have been working hard on a project or with a group, we can feel hard done by when our contribution is not fully appreciated. Direct criticism can be painful. But the harder the message, the more important it can be. Sometimes we delude ourselves and need to hear the truth. Sometimes we need to accept that we are not going to progress any further in terms of promotion or that a relationship is not going to be redeemed. Accepting the hard reality of our limitations is difficult, but it is folly to ignore the message. Accepting hard messages can sometimes take us to insights about ourselves that build new confidence which is more realistic and sustaining.

Brian's story

Brian had entered his organization as a bright graduate. His intellectual strengths and ability to get things done had impressed his bosses. He moved rapidly from one difficult assignment to another and kept being promoted. By his mid-30s he had been promoted into a leadership role.

He was good at getting things done by virtue of his own energy and effort. But switching into a leadership role meant that he needed to use the resources of others rather than do everything himself. His first reaction was to try to do everything himself, which did not go down well with his staff or some of his peers. Eventually his boss had to sit him down and give him some hard messages about using the resources in his team effectively and not trying to do everything himself. At first Brian resented this direct challenge from his boss: he had never been spoken to like this before. He had to use a different repertoire of skills to get things done. He needed to build a different quality of relationship with his staff. He began to accept that he should be much more rigorous about where he was adding value and where others could take forward action without his being involved.

The weeks after the tough talking-to by his boss were perhaps the most formative weeks in his life. Initially he accepted intellectually that he needed to change his approach. Accepting the need to change emotionally was more difficult, but he got feedback from his direct reports, was deliberate in changing his approach, became much more effective as a leader as a consequence and went on to more senior posts within his chosen sphere. He was for ever grateful that he had been given hard messages by his boss and that he had allowed those messages to change his approach radically.

Hard messages can hit us in a variety of ways. They can be tough words from a boss or feedback from staff or observations from our family. There can be hard messages when we see pain or tragedy either in our personal lives or in our community. Hard messages can be about living with our weaknesses and acknowledging that we are never going to achieve all that we might have set out to do.

Understanding what you are less good at

Understanding and being honest about your least strong areas is crucial to making progress. Pretending that your least strong areas do not exist might work in the short term but is folly in the long term. Understanding what we are less good at involves:

- Being honest with ourselves
- Understanding the reasons we are less strong in some areas than in others
- Being clear about the mismatch between the expectations upon us at work, at home or in the community and the mix of strengths and less strong areas that we bring
- Being clear how we would like to develop these less strong areas and about the steps we are going to take
- Getting feedback from others on our progress and rewarding ourselves when we achieve certain steps

In their book *Now, Discover Your Strengths*, Marcus Buckingham and Donald O. Clifton talk about a weakness as "anything that gets in the way of excellent performance." They discuss five creative strategies for handling weaknesses:

- *Get a little better at it.* This might not sound very ambitious, but in some instances it is the only workable strategy.

- ◼ *Design a support system.* Ensure there are people around you who complement your particular contribution.
- ◼ *Use one of your strongest themes to overwhelm your weakness.*
- ◼ *Find a partner.* Team up with another individual to bring a complementary approach.
- ◼ *Just stop doing.* This might be a strategy of last resort, but when it is used it can be empowering.

Sometimes the answer is to reframe what some regard as a weakness as a strength. For example, some people might criticize you for delaying making a decision when in fact you are good at waiting for the right moment to be decisive. Some might see you as too soft-hearted when you are in fact maximizing your understanding of how people are reacting in a particular situation.

Sandra has an impressive set of strengths. She likes persuading people. She is decisive and inquisitive. She does not get bogged down in detail. She is comfortable dealing with a variety of issues at the same time and good at injecting creativity. She likes dealing with new problems and is future oriented. Her family see her strengths as having energy and enthusiasm and as being creative, always supportive, a good organizer and happy to share.

Sandra acknowledges, however, that there are things she is less good at. She acknowledges that she is not good at detailed, forensic assessment of evidence. She can be overly enthusiastic. She does not think she is at her best in jobs which involve a lot of processes. She can take on too much. Sometimes the best can be the enemy of the good. She does not always relax as much as she should.

When Sandra went into a new role after a promotion it was an excellent time to take stock of her strengths and her less strong areas. She knew that she had to face up to her less strong areas. She had huge strengths that were the foundation of her success in her new leadership role. But she was conscious that she had to accept hard messages about needing to change certain aspects of her approach. She recognized that it was not a matter of changing her basic personality. There was an essential "Sandra-ness" in her that was crucial to her success. Her energy and enthusiasm were infectious and needed to continue to be there, but she recognized that she had to use the skills of others even better. She needed to prioritize her time so that her focus was on what only she could do, without getting too involved in every area.

Sandra had a strong intent to take an effective step up into her new role. This was exactly the moment to take the hard messages on board and adapt her approach, which she did with considerable success. But it did mean facing up to some hard messages.

Donald was always regarded as pragmatic and as having good project management skills. He always brought a good delivery focus and was excellent at getting to solutions. He was driven to get on with things and was clear what he wanted from other people. Donald acknowledged his less strong points, which included getting nervous when presenting to a wider group. He could be intolerant with people who did not see his point, and he could write people off. He was sometimes less strong on the detail and could gloss over certain key elements.

What worked for Donald was a step-by-step approach. This involved taking one point at a time, observing himself to see when he was less effective and when he was trying out different approaches. First he addressed being nervous when presenting to a wider group; he did more thorough preparation and thought himself into the role more. The result was good feedback for his presentations. Second he tackled becoming more aware when he was intolerant of people; he consciously decided to be friendly and encouraging with people who annoyed him. This step-by-step approach helped Donald build greater confidence in the areas where he was receiving hard messages. It was not necessarily a quick process, but he was confident that he was taking the right steps and was receiving feedback that indicated progress was being made.

Each of us receives hard messages on a regular basis. It is quite right to ignore some of these messages when they say far more about the individual giving them than about the recipient. Sometimes a hard message is about something that is not going to change because of the nature of our personality. But on many occasions hard messages call out for self-reflection and working through to a thoughtful and considered response.

Questions to ask yourself might be:

- What hard messages have I received in the past few weeks?
- Which of those hard messages do I want to do something about?
- What are my next steps in addressing a couple of those messages?
- What would be a successful outcome?

Watching self-delusions

Giles always saw himself as the best lawyer in the practice, and he frequently had repeat business. He had his own way of doing things, which for many years had proved successful. But all of a sudden the number of clients approaching him began to drop off. He still thought that he was the most effective lawyer in the practice, but no one else was referring business to him. Rather reluctantly he began to ask why the number of clients he had was declining. The feedback, which was not easy to obtain, was about a touch of arrogance and a slight datedness in his approach.

For many years Giles had been deluding himself that he was a cut above the other lawyers in the practice. Perhaps he was, intellectually, but in terms of current credibility, there were beginning to be some question marks. Facing up to the hard messages given gently by one or two of his colleagues made Giles realize that he had been deluding himself and that he needed to take action. Fortunately, it was not too late to remedy the situation, and he was soon back up to a full list of clients.

Sometimes we need to delude ourselves. Our survival in some situations depends on blanking out certain elements of truth and being focused on one or two essential outcomes. But if we delude ourselves for too long our blindness to reality can be our undoing.

Have there been times when you were deluding yourself? Maybe for a short period this was necessary. But sometimes a hard message that we have been deluding ourselves is essential to our coming back to reality and adjusting our approach and behavior to meet new expectations.

When you are hit by personal tragedy

Many people will admit to a friend that moments of personal tragedy have been among the most important influences upon them. Jeremy was a successful Chief Executive. For him a defining moment was when he had seen his mother killed in a car crash many years ago. How he coped with that tragic situation made him the person he is. Keeping going when he was gripped with grief and personal pain gave him a strength of character that took him through many different situations as a leader.

Malcolm talks of when a colleague phoned to say he was going to meet him and died in a car crash on the journey there. The outcome for Malcolm was that he treasures friendships and always builds personal warmth into constructive working relationships, which he tends with care.

The hard shocks that come from tragedy in our personal lives can reinforce what is most important to us and often provide a strong motivation to make a difference in our working lives.

Questions to ask yourself might be:

- Which tragic moments have had a formative influence upon me?
- How do those tragic moments feed through to my current values and attitudes?
- How often do I share my learning from tragic moments as a means of encouraging others?

Realizing that you will go no further

Miranda taught in a sixth form college. She had been promoted to Head of Department but ideally wanted to become part of the senior management team. She had a strong track record of success. Her department was popular with students because it was creative and because students got good grades at the end of their studies. She wanted the status of being part of the senior management team, but corporate leadership was not necessarily her natural home.

For a long while Miranda was determined to get promoted. The Principal sat her down one day; he was very complimentary about her leadership of the department but said that frankly he did not see her as a member of the senior management team. He put across his message thoughtfully and sensitively, but it was a hard message for Miranda to take. She was grumpy about it at first, but after a while she recognized the reality of the situation. She began to acknowledge to herself that she would continue to enjoy her work as Head of Department, whereas she was not sure how much she would enjoy the responsibilities of corporate leadership. It was a hard message for Miranda but one she knew she had to accept.

Are there any resonances for you with hard messages concerning limitations on your own career advancement? Sometimes we need to accept what we are good at and then recognize that others are better suited to more senior roles. Part of success for Miranda was accepting that she could make a big difference as Head of Department and did not need the status or authority of becoming a member of the senior management team to have a fulfilled and influential impact within the college.

Acknowledging that your area of work is going nowhere

Martin had built a career in supply change management. He had taken forward a range of successful assignments and was highly thought of.

But the market for supply change managers began to diminish. The effect of much more sophisticated software was that the types of skill supply change managers needed were changing. He was gradually feeling out of date, and he was getting fewer and fewer contracts.

His first reaction was to fight on and demonstrate that he had valuable skills. This worked for a while, but the reality of the changing market was against him. He could not change the world single-handedly. Martin was blinkered and found it difficult to face up to the reality of the changing situation for his profession.

It took repeated frankness from some of his friends for Martin to begin to realize that he had to change his approach. He began to think about moving into teaching, but that did not resonate with him. He thought through working in the voluntary sector but was put off by the low pay that he would be able to obtain there. He was feeling a bit stuck and only slowly accepting the reality of his situation. The hard messages were taking quite a time to sink in. He was having difficulty adjusting to a new reality and only reluctantly admitted he would need to seek another type of work or retire.

Accepting that you are in a working relationship that is not going to change

Many of us believe that we are influential and can always build new relationships with different people. We have a belief that we can work effectively with anyone. It is then a rude awakening when we find that a working relationship is going nowhere. We try different approaches; we try to build a common cause, develop a clearer understanding of where the individual is coming from and be encouraging. But it is as if we are banging our head against a brick wall. There seems to be no progress at all.

It can be a hard message when we are not able to turn somebody around to our way of thinking.

Alan had worked successfully with a number of Secretaries of State, but then he began to work with one with whom the chemistry did not seem to be effective at all. This was hard for Alan to take as he had prided himself on building excellent relationships with his political masters. Gradually he accepted that he would need to move on, and he did so, initially with some reluctance. For Alan this experience of recognizing the reality of a relationship that was not going to improve helped him move into a more realistic place.

The hard message that this relationship was not going to work did not stop Alan from aiming to make other relationships work effectively.

But it did mean he developed a greater sense of the reality that sometimes relationships work effectively but on other occasions the hard truth is that a relationship is not that productive and is unlikely to be so.

Accepting the reality of hard messages

Perhaps there have been occasions when you have had to accept the reality of hard messages. It has been a defining moment that you are not going to progress further or that the area of work you are involved in is going nowhere or that a difficult relationship is not going to be redeemed. Accepting the reality of a hard message is part of our continually growing up. Stark truth is always painful, but it toughens us up and makes us the people we are.

Next steps

Accepting the truth of hard messages is always painful. When we stop beating our head against a brick wall there can be a sense of liberation and moving on. The truth of unwelcome hard messages can enable us to shift our perspective and our life and career journey constructively.

Questions to ask yourself might be:

■ Which hard messages have been the most painful to receive?
■ As a result of hard messages, how willing have I been to change my approach as a leader?
■ How willing am I to face up to hard messages in the future?
■ Do I always invite people to give me the hard messages I need to hear?
■ What is a hard message I have received recently which I should be addressing?

12 Embedding learning moments

Our lives are full of learning moments; some we dismiss, some we are unaware of, and others we treasure. In our childhood there were learning moments every day. In adulthood the number of learning moments might diminish to a trickle. But there are times when we are taken aback by our own learning, which might be learning about ourselves, from others, from individual projects, about what we do best or from our own career. Keeping up the flow of learning moments can help us stay fresh. As soon as we stop learning our horizons can close in on us, our confidence can diminish, and our attitudes become much more small-minded.

Gillian's story

Gillian was preoccupied with her own reputation. She was for ever thinking about whom she could impress. Her preoccupation was with building a reputation for responsiveness in getting things done. This meant that she was constantly jumping from one task to another. There was always the danger of the latest request trumping earlier requests so that life was full of three-quarters-finished tasks.

Gillian's concern with building her reputation by being responsive led to her getting a reputation for failing to complete what she had committed herself to do. The more she tried to build her reputation, the more tarnished it became. She went off work sick with stress and with a list of uncompleted remits.

As she began to recover at home Gillian became increasingly clear that she needed to learn from her folly. The first step was to understand the cycle she was caught in. She began to recognize that she needed to be more disciplined in completing tasks and limit her willingness to take on other remits until she had completed what she had already committed herself to do. This was a painful period of readjustment. She embedded the learning about herself and thought clearly about how she was going to handle her search for a positive reputation in the future.

> After she returned to work Gillian was much more methodical. There was always a risk of her wanting to please. But she knew that she had to be more structured in her use of time and energy, and she managed to keep up a reasonable discipline in the remits she accepted from others.

Learning comes in many different ways. It can be learning about yourself, learning from others, learning from individual projects, learning from when you are at your best and learning from your career. It can also be learning from understanding the significance of particular events and taking stock at the end of a day or a month.

Learning about yourself

When Sylvia took on heading a major review there were many pluses about the exercise. She learned a great deal about a new sector and about the best way of conducting a major review. Sylvia also acknowledged that she had learned a lot about herself in the process:

- She should have managed her team more proactively.
- She should have been clearer to herself about the unique value she was bringing to the role.
- She should have had brainstorming conversations earlier on about some of the main issues.
- She should have ensured there was a summary of an emerging way forward at an early stage.

Sylvia also learned through the process that the political skills she brought to this role were valuable. The learning was both the recognition of strengths she brought to this demanding review and the need to set up the arrangements for any future review in a rather different way.

What Sylvia learned about herself was that when she moved to a different type of activity she needed to re-evaluate her approach and adapt it to the new set of circumstances. A leadership approach that had worked well in one context was not necessarily immediately transferable to another. Adaptation to a new role and new people was important. The over-arching lesson was to be continually alert to learning about yourself as you move from one leadership situation to another.

Learning from others

Other people are always fascinating to watch. We can learn from what others do well or less well. Observing others can give us new insights. When Stan reflected about his boss he was clear what he wanted to gain in terms of learning from her. He wanted to learn from her ability to handle herself well with the Chair, her confidence in her ability to deliver and her ability to listen well. We reflected on those aspects of her behavior he wanted to embrace in his own approach so that his reputation for listening and his confidence about delivering would grow. This was not about mimicking his boss but about analyzing carefully which aspects of another person's style worked well and which aspects might be built into his own leadership repertoire.

Questions to ask might be:

- Which leaders do I particularly admire?
- What is the learning I want to embrace from them?
- What are the distinctive aspects of their approach I feel able to embed in my own good practice?

Learning from when you are at your best

Thomas was uncertain about how best to move on. He had just been for an interview and knew that his performance had not been that good. This had sapped his confidence and put him in an uneasy type of limbo.

Thomas and I began to work through how he had handled situations when he had been at his best. He said that he was most effective when he felt confident and self-assured. His emotional wellbeing was particularly important to him in dealing with intellectually difficult issues well. If life was good at home he brought to his work a positive energy which enabled him to see how problems could be solved.

What he recognized less readily was that he was also good at dealing with subjects that he did not know well. He had a track record of moving from one area of responsibility to another. As long as he was feeling confident, he could crack new issues with purpose and skill. For Thomas it was a crucial learning moment when he took stock after not getting the interview right. The learning was about being prepared emotionally for tough situations. He had not been properly prepared for the interview and it had gone wrong. The experience reinforced the importance of being prepared emotionally for difficult situations so that he had reserves of confidence to deal with whatever was thrown at him.

Whenever we give a presentation or chair a meeting and it goes well, it is invaluable to take stock and reflect on why it went well and what we can learn from it. Too easily we enjoy the words of praise but then move quickly on. If someone gives you positive feedback that is general, it can be valuable to ask that they be more specific so that you are sure what worked really well and therefore which element of learning you need to embed.

It is about celebrating with a purpose and saying, "Great, that went well," but then reflecting on the two or three key points that need now to become part of your normal approach.

Good questions to ask yourself on a regular basis are:

- What has gone really well in the past couple of weeks?
- What were the particular features of what I did that made it go well?
- What is the resultant learning that I want to embed?

Learning from individual projects

Philip led a sequence of projects for a major management consultancy. After completing one project, he described it as a defining moment to take stock of his learning. He had learned a lot about the firm, the commercial aspects, the opportunity costs, the way the team had worked together, the needs of clients and his own reactions. The learning related to individual components, but most of all he had learned a new approach to holding a big project together. The learning was about standing above the individual components and ensuring the strategy held true and was taken forward effectively to the next level.

This was an illustration for Philip that you can embed learning at different levels. At one level it is about technical skills, and at another level it is about your ability to hold together disparate interests and different sets of priorities.

Learning from your own career

I often invite people to look back and see the pattern of their learning from different parts of their career. Toni talked about learning from a period of secondment that she was tougher than she thought. She learned that she could always be clear about finding a way forward, that she could be forensic when she needed to be, that effective preparation on technical issues was vital and that it was important to identify and unlock personal agendas.

Toni also talked about the learning from working with an individual who was not easy. What worked for Toni was being clear on the overall objectives, not getting bogged down, working carefully through the next steps and making clear that she was there to ensure a successful outcome.

The testimony of many leaders in that at each stage in their career there have been crucial learning moments. Embedding those learning moments has helped them move on to be more effective senior leaders and make a step-change in terms of their strategic impact.

The value of taking stock regularly

At the end of a training event participants can be asked to write on a postcard two or three points which they have learned and then to look again at that postcard in three months' time. This simple device can provide a means of summarizing our learning (because it has to fit on a postcard) and reminding ourselves of the learning by looking at the postcard after some time has elapsed. Some organizations collect the postcards and then send them to individuals three months after the event.

It is helpful to ask yourself at the end of each week:

■ What are the nuggets of learning from this week?
■ Which aspects of the learning have been completely new?
■ Which element of the leaning is a reinforcement of what I know already?
■ How best can I build that learning into my next steps?

Learning moments can be insignificant small steps or major, life-changing switches of direction. Sometimes we have learned a lot gradually without fully recognizing the change. On other occasions the learning is dramatic and life-changing. Graeme had been gradually building up his confidence in speaking at big conferences; there was a eureka moment when he got extremely positive feedback and recognized that he had been able to change people's perspectives on a complex legal issue. He had learned how to influence and persuade a major audience effectively and was delighted with his learning.

Next steps

Being clear what our learning moments have been and how they have made us the people we are can be significant. Keeping up learning moments whatever our age is essential to staying fresh and creative.

Key questions to ask yourself might be:

- What are the learning moments that have been most important to me in my life?
- How readily did I embed learning from those moments?
- What have been the most important learning moments over the past 12 months?
- How do I ensure a continuous flow of learning moments in the future?
- What is my current focus of learning?

SECTION F

Capturing the moment

This section is about how we capture the moment. Sometimes these are positive moments which take us into a new way of thinking. On other occasions they can involve taking a deep breath and taking necessary action which is painful.

This section looks it turn at:

- Creative moments
- Gripping the moment
- Living with discord

Often we meander through time. Sometimes it takes a lot of energy to generate creative moments, grip a difficult moment or live with discord in an effective way. This section deals with some of the tougher aspects of how we use time which can make our brain hurt or test the strength of our resolve.

13 Creative moments

When are we at our most creative? Who stimulates us effectively to think in new ways? Creativity is not just for the artist or the musician. We can often be doing a task in a routine way and not be alert to different ways of tackling it. When someone is creative, we might dismiss their idea as irrelevant. But how can we be more creative and use those creative moments to best effect?

Salim's story

Salim was wrestling with the best way of marketing a particular book. He had obtained excellent written material from the author and had put together a press release which he thought worked well. His colleagues were concerned that the language he had used was dull and repetitive. They did not think it would catch anyone's imagination. Salim was initially deflated by their reaction.

He decided that he needed to be more creative. He looked out some of the press releases that he had always regarded as most effective. He tried to stand in the shoes of his readers. He crystallized more clearly than before some of the messages he wanted to get across. The result was a press release and other material that was sharper, more passionate and more relevant to the people he was addressing.

He had forced himself to be creative and was happy with his output. He was determined to keep up this quality on future projects. He knew that being creative gave him energy. He was determined not to get bogged down in future.

Creative moments can be times when we think clearly, when we draw analogies well, when we give tough feedback, when we are looking into the next phase of our life or when we are stretching ourselves.

When are you at your most creative?

Each of us has creative moments when we think in different ways. I am at my most creative either when going into London on a train or when walking at the weekend. What works best for me is jotting down ideas on a sheet of paper and then trying to link those ideas together. There are a number of people with whom I know I will have creative conversations. When Robin Linnecar and I wrote the book *Business Coaching* we had some superbly creative conversations about what we would write in each chapter. One of the pleasures of the book I am writing on effective teams is the joint endeavor of thinking through different aspects with my co-author, Judy Hirst.

The time and space when you are at your most creative is precious. For Ben it is 2:00 a.m. in the morning, for Anthea it is when she is riding her bicycle to work, for Bethany it is after the children have gone to sleep, for Henry it is while he is swimming, for Mushtak it is while he is at the mosque and for Reg it is while he is kicking a football with other members of the Veterans' team.

As you look back over the past year, ask yourself:

- What have been my most creative moments?
- Were they part of a regular pattern or were they unplanned?
- What is the rhythm of creative moments that works best for me?

Creating moments to think

Nancy Kline, in her book *Time to Think*, talks of the 10 components of a thinking environment. These are:

- *Attention*: listening with respect and interest
- *Incisive questions*: removing assumptions that limit ideas
- *Equality*: treating each other as thinking peers, giving equal terms and attention, and keeping agreements and boundaries
- *Appreciation*: practicing a five-to-one ratio of appreciation to criticism
- *Ease*: offering freedom from rush or urgency
- *Encouragement*: moving beyond competition
- *Feelings*: allowing sufficient emotional release to restore thinking
- *Information*: providing a full and accurate picture of reality
- *Place*: creating a physical environment that says back to people, "You matter"
- *Diversity*: adding quality because of the differences between us

What can help us think clearly is the quality of attention we are able to give to an issue, the incisiveness of the questions we ask ourselves and the quality of the dialogue with others. As soon as appreciation and encouragement replace competition we can move into a creative space that allows us to bounce ideas off each other and move into a much more productive process of thinking together.

The power of drawing analogies

Drawing analogies between a work activity and an area of personal interest can be powerful. For Tom the interaction between his approach to his work and his approach to photography provided a rich stimulus to become more creative in both spheres.

As a serious amateur photographer, Tom was passionate about developing his skills. He had created exhibitions which had been acclaimed. He was much more in control of the camera. What mattered most to him was the standard of the pictures he took and not necessarily whether they were on the front page of a particular website. He wanted to continue learning how to take really good pictures. He wanted to ensure he could finesse the level of blurredness to maximize the impact of individual pictures.

In his photography he was increasingly creative and he was growing in confidence. He set up a new site, which many people visited. He was engaging with other people and collaborating with them. He was continually developing his skills. He was taking criticism from others about his photography positively and continuing to refine the quality of his photographs.

For Tom the parallels with his work were clear: he was continuing to grow in self-confidence and develop his skill set. Finessing the level of blurredness in his photographs was akin to living with ambiguity in his work situation. He was advocating what he did within his organization in new ways. He was enjoying engaging with other colleagues even more and being creative in the work they did together.

For Tom the more he did with his photography in terms of pushing the boundaries of creativity, the more this led straight back into his work. The photography was not an irrelevant diversion; it was fundamental to Tom growing his skills and confidence in his own ability and judgment, which reinforced those same generic qualities in the working environment.

When I wrote the book *The Four Vs of Leadership: Vision, Values, Value-added and Vitality*, the theme that resonated most with people was vitality. The question at the heart of my approach was, Whatever gives you energy, can you do more of it? Whatever activity engages us in our personal lives is likely to be a prime source of creativity, whether this activity is physical, intellectual, emotional or spiritual. The more creative we are in our personal lives, the more that creativity will feed back into the work environment.

May I invite you to reflect on:

- Which activities generate most creativity for me?
- How can I best learn from that creativity and transfer some of the confidence and skills into other aspects of my life?

Giving tough feedback

A number of people say that some of their most creative moments have been when they were giving tough feedback to others. When Paul took on one leadership role he knew he would need to have conversations with a particular colleague. Being part of tough conversations with this colleague was when Paul felt he came of age. Having handled these conversations well, he did not fear the prospect of similar conversations in the future. Before, he had always needed approval and praise prior to taking tough action. Now he was much more willing to take necessary steps and to risk disharmony.

In certain areas of his life Paul could be assertive, but in some environments he seemed to lose confidence and was not so effective. Paul concluded that the difference had something to do with being shy with particular people. As soon as he had upped the quality of his interaction with different individuals and been prepared to express tough views, there was a breakthrough and he was in a much stronger frame of mind.

Gerald had always been regarded as a high-flyer. His mind worked quickly, and he was able to produce radical solutions that worked. But there was a reluctance to have hard conversations. He was conscious that this was a legacy from his background. In one job he knew he had to ask three people to leave the organization. He prepared long and hard, got excellent advice and had the critical conversations thoughtfully and effectively. The three people left, and the organization quickly responded well.

For Gerald taking forward these difficult conversations had been cathartic. He now knew that he could do difficult conversations. Exiting these three people had been tough and necessary, but it was a creative moment for Gerald in releasing him from his previous inhibitions and liberating him to have tough conversations when they were required.

Thinking creatively about handling a job well

When I reconnected with Iain after two-and-a-half years we did a stocktake of what he had been learning. Iain said:

■ I feel much more positive about my current responsibilities.
■ I feel I understand much more about effective leadership.
■ I have felt much more on top of my brief in the past year.
■ I am much better at prioritizing in the moment and making decisions, and I am becoming better at dealing with people.
■ I feel stronger and more resilient.
■ I feel I have grown up a lot in the past year.

The foundation of being creative about the future was being clear about what he had learned over the previous year or two. We then focused on areas where he wanted to be more creative in the future:

■ Developing his public speaking skills
■ Raising his profile in different sorts of meeting
■ Thinking through creatively different options for the future

The process of crystallizing his learning enabled Iain to establish an ambitious set of aspirations for his next phase. He tried out different ways of contributing creatively in meetings and speaking at public events. He was thrilled by his own progress and reveled in the creativity that he was now able to use.

An excellent way of creating moments of creativity is to do a stocktake of what has gone well and use that as the basis for deciding on two or three areas where you want to develop your skills further. This is about establishing a secure basis from which to push the boundaries of your creativity outward.

Looking into the next phase of life

Reaching significant ages can provide a good basis for taking stock of how you want to be creative in the future. I met Rob on the day he turned 50. I encouraged him to sit in the post-50 chair and say what he liked about the pre-50 person. He said:

■ I really like your sense of humor.
■ I like your diverse range of interests.

- I like the ambition that has got you here and I like the can-do attitude.
- I like the way you have developed better judgment so that you are not so arrogant.
- You have set me up well for my post-50 years, and I have the potential to enjoy a lot of freedom.
- I like the way you are willing to be unconventional.

But he also said to the pre-50 self:

- I am leaving the chip behind.
- I am leaving behind an earlier definition of ambition.
- I am leaving behind my temper.

Sitting in the post-50 seat Rob said to his pre-50 self that he was not different in a number of ways:

- I am happy in the skin I'm in.
- I don't have a need to be somewhere else.
- I am determined to enjoy life more.
- I am rapidly becoming more aware of how a broad population of people see me.
- The more I get into things, the happier I am.
- I intend to liberate myself and be comfortable doing so.

Rob then sat in the pre-50 chair and gave the following advice to his post-50 self:

- Do not get bogged down: I have wasted a lot of time in the past.
- Concentrate on the value-added of what you can do.
- Do not try to do it all.
- Do not succumb to the wrong sort of peer pressure.
- Identify where you can make more impact in things outside the office.
- Do not let the things you value be undermined.

Rob then reflected on where he wanted to be in three or four years' time and said that the perspective he wanted then was to be able to say:

- I have made a difference in the areas that are most important to me.
- I continue to be comfortable in the skin I am in.

■ I have moved on in terms of my next steps, and I am clear about what the next steps in my life are to be.

For Rob this was a very creative moment, on his 50th birthday looking backward and forward. The simple device of the post-50 person talking to the pre-50 person helped crystallize a lot of the learning and next steps.

Whenever we reach a significant birthday or anniversary, it can be a creative moment to look backward and forward. This is about embedding what is precious to us and then being willing to step into the future positively and creatively.

Knowing the best ways in which to stretch yourself

Being creative isn't necessarily doing something radically different. It can be using current skills and gifts to even better effect. For the footballer who can kick a good free kick which tests the goalkeeper, being creative might be bending the ball even more through the air. In this case, creativity is developing a skill further rather than developing a new skill altogether.

Chris had moved successfully into a big Director role. He had developed a range of skills which meant he had an influential contribution to make across the organization. Being creative for Chris was not about being radically different. It was about using his influencing skills even more effectively with a wider range of people. It was using his skills with his stakeholders to understand their perspective and provide a clear way forward.

Being creative for the sake of doing something different can be a diversion. Using existing skills ever more creatively can provide an excellent platform for success.

Next steps

Knowing when you are at your most creative is a special gift. Establishing a pattern which enables you to be creative on a regular basis keeps you fresh and moving on. Being creative is not necessarily being radically different. It might be adapting your repertoire to good effect when you have built a clear understanding about both yourself and the context within which you are working.

Questions to reflect on might be:

- When have I been most creative in the past?
- At what time of the week or day am I most creative?
- Can I stretch my creativity in new ways?
- What are the creative moments I need to ensure happen over the next few weeks?
- What areas of my personal interests can I develop further where I can grow my creativity?

14 Gripping the moment

The eagle flies gracefully in the sky, and then all of a sudden it swoops down on its prey. In an instant the graceful flying has become a powerful dive that ends in a tight grip on the prey. The eagle chooses its moment and then grips intensely. If we tried to grip every moment we would be exhausted. But which moments do we grip, and how do we ensure that there is a coherence in what we focus on? It is the moments that we grip that often change our lives.

Bob's story

Bob was a genial manager who liked to work by consensus. He had a generous-hearted approach, and his staff were loyal to him. But he was sometimes regarded as too easy-going.

The feedback from his boss and others was that sometimes he needed to get a grip. His personality made him reluctant to rush in with hobnailed boots, but he recognized that there was a valid point in the criticisms he was receiving. He knew that he could not go on as he was. When a major problem occurred he decided to take control. He used his authority to ensure certain things happened. He took a grip in a way which was assertive without being aggressive. Staff and colleagues responded well. They appreciated his attempt to get a grip. He felt that he had made a step-change in his approach and was grateful for the recognition from those around him.

Gripping a moment can have many elements. It can be gripping yourself, your job, the action, opportunities or next steps. Gripping the action is about being in control and not being in the grip, when you are out of control.

Gripping yourself

Colin had been through a tough time. His most recent job had not worked out as well as he had hoped. He was now in a new role, his smile was back, and this new job had restored his self-confidence. On occasion in his previous role he had been caught in the crossfire. In the new role he was determined to keep a grip on himself. He talked about being explicit with himself about the facts, telling himself the right stories to stay positive, being honest when there was an error of judgment, forgiving himself and not beating himself up after he had made a genuine mistake, and moving on rather than getting bogged down in single difficult issues. His boss had said he was glad that Colin was on the team; he was getting into his stride. He was looking forward to the opportunities that the job would bring.

After a time of uncertainty Colin felt that he was making progress. This progress was both about using his time well and about getting a grip on his own emotions. Sometimes apprehension or uncertainty had meant he became stuck. He felt he now had enough control over himself to be decisive and positive in his actions. The more confident about himself Colin became, the more he was able to handle difficult problems well. There was now a strong sense of movement forward.

How often do we tell ourselves to get a grip? Sometimes these are gentle words of motivation. On other occasions they are a stern message we are giving ourselves. When we try to grip ourselves we can easily slip out of the grip, as we know all the best ways of deluding ourselves. Sometimes it is a matter of laughing at ourselves as we try to slither out of the grip.

Gripping your job

Jennifer was getting enormous pleasure out of her new role. Her previous role had not been the success she had wanted, but in this job she was able to say, "I set the agenda, I have taken what was there and molded it, I am articulating better to others what needs to be done, and I am using my background and skills effectively." She got strong endorsement from the Chief Executive. This encouragement helped her to move on from being vulnerable and uncertain, and it helped her grow back her confidence. She was investing in a job that was worthwhile, and she was making a massive difference.

After a difficult period in her previous role she had wondered whether she would be able to grip a job successfully again. But the success of this role renewed the confidence within her and enabled her to believe that she could handle future demands successfully.

Gripping the action

Brenda had moved to a very different role which involved executive responsibility for a major program of work. She had spent a few months learning the context and was now determined to make a positive difference. She was conscious that she needed to:

■ Put clear milestones in the ground about what was acceptable and unacceptable behavior
■ Make tough decisions about individuals, if necessary
■ Be authoritative without being aggressive
■ Continue to listen hard while bringing wider perspectives into her contributions
■ Watch out if she became disengaged or difficult

Certain individuals were testing her resolve. She was conscious that she needed to come out in control, but she did not want to create a situation that resulted in difficult personal relationships. As she was seen to grip the action successfully, those who had been testing her out saw the merit of her approach and became some of her biggest allies.

Gripping the action is easiest when everybody is on board. Sometimes you cannot wait that long. Getting a grip might mean taking charge when some people are uncertain. It can take time to get some people on board; sometimes they have to be dragged along with the others. A good sense of timing is important in judging when others, albeit reluctantly, will acquiesce in the action you take.

There is a point in every new role when action can wait no longer. A difficult problem has to be gripped or a financial gap has to be tackled. We sometimes fear rushing in where angels fear to tread, and we want time to be assured about the right approach. But that assurance is not always something we are given.

When Julie began a new role she spent time talking to the staff, listening to customers and building a relationship with key stakeholders. It was pointed criticism of aspects of the organization from a non-executive director that pushed her to a place where she knew she had to take action. She got to grip with key figures and understood the trends. But fairly rapidly she recognized that big decisions were needed about priorities. She was hesitant to propose drastic changes to the existing priorities on the basis of limited experience. She tested her ideas out with people she trusted. She became increasingly confident that her instincts were right. She put together a clear plan for the next couple of years. She shared it in draft with her colleagues, who were impressed by her insight and accepted that action was unavoidable.

Julie knew what to do, even though it felt like jumping off a cliff. By taking the action she did, she turned the organization around, and she was grateful that she had followed her own judgment and allowed the criticism of the non-executive director to push her over the edge.

When you are starting a new job it is often useful to have points at which you take stock and review. To ask yourself at the three-month or six-month point "What do I need to get a grip on?" can be a valuable discipline.

Gripping a current opportunity

Heather talks about being blessed by the opportunity to focus in the moment. She is single-minded, and a sense of independence is important to her. When she sees an opportunity she is always up for gripping the moment. She can get excited in the moment, and she tends to want to do something quickly. She uses the approach of having conversations with imaginary people who help her put the opportunity into context.

In the excitement of the moment there is sometimes a risk of acting too quickly – hence the value of slowing down and being measured about whether action now is right. Sometimes conversations in your head can help you decide whether gripping a moment is appropriate or whether it is time to take stock and not rush in a particular decision.

Gripping next steps

Sometimes your current role can feel comfortable. You are learning a lot and there is no real need to move on. But life is often not that straightforward. You are doing a job well and being appreciated, and then all of a sudden circumstances change and you are a voice of the past not the future.

Staying alert to next steps is not only about keeping up our motivation; it is about being alert as to when is the right time to move on. When Henry took stock it was clear that he had been doing a good job; he was altering the expectations of others and ensuring that change took place effectively. Henry's work in the organization had helped him develop toughness because he had to think independently. But he knew it would be time to move on within 12 months or so. It was time to grip his own future, which meant thinking hard about where he wanted to go next, building new relationships, clarifying the skills that he wanted to bring to his next role and loosening some of the emotional ties in his current role. Beginning to grip his next steps meant loosening the grip in his current role. He began to accept change and was looking forward to moving on.

Sometimes situations can drift. What was a mild problem gradually becomes a significant one. For example, deaths in a hospital are inevitable. Spotting trends is important to determine whether the pattern of deaths is becoming out of the ordinary. Early action, before a trend turns into a crisis, can make a huge difference.

Seeing a trend and then gripping the action early requires good data and a reflective approach that means you are not caught in a cycle of self-deception.

Gripping the present

Sometimes we close our ears when someone we do not fully respect is speaking. We assume their comments will be rubbish and therefore do not listen to them. But others might be swayed by their reflections.

Gripping the present is about treating the words of anyone who speaks on their merits and not being too influenced by whether we like the speaker. Truth is spoken by many people, not just those we like. When we feel distracted, gripping ourselves so that we stay in the present can be important to ensure we do not miss nuggets of truth.

Gripping ourselves might sometimes be about pinching ourselves so that we stay alert. It can be about not writing people off. It is recognizing the truth in what people say so that we grip the present and understand its significance and build upon it.

Gripping future moments

Our own experience of gripping moments in the past informs us how to do that best in the future. Knowing when to have a loose hold, when to watch as others grip an issue and when to grip it ourselves is part of the difficult task of leadership. We can only ever grip a limited number of issues at the same time. It can be worth reflecting on:

- What are the current issues I need to get a grip on?
- Which of those issues is it for me grip rather than somebody else?
- How best do I get a grip on issues which I do not enjoy handling?

Next steps

We take satisfaction in observing others grip a moment well. There will be times in our own experience when we have got a grip and it has worked well. But there might be circumstances now when we need to get a grip even though it feels uncomfortable.

Questions to reflect on might be:

- Which situation am I most pleased about having got a grip on?
- What have I learned about people who have got a grip on issues successfully?
- What are the current opportunities I need to grip?
- How best do I grip myself to stay in the present and not write off the contributions of others?
- What things do I need to let go of and not grip?

15 Living with discord

Our ideal is to live in harmony. The Hebrew word "shalom" is not about a gentle peace but about living together in harmony. But discord is part of life. Without discord at work there would be no creative tension. Without discord in our personal lives there would be no character and limited creativity. Sometimes discord is an inevitable evil. Sometimes discord can bring out the best out in us.

Naomi's story

Naomi had a busy life balancing work and home. She had to deal with discord at work, where she was involved with a controversial piece of legislation and faced repeated buffeting from groups critical of the intention of the legislation. There was discord at home because of the conflicting priorities of Naomi and her husband and the demands of two teenage children. Living with discord was what Naomi did, and she was pretty good at it. Naomi compartmentalized her life and was not fazed by difficult conversations either at work or at home. She had developed a protective skin which served her well in many respects. But at work it became clear that it did not really matter to her whether she upset people with her single-mindedness. At home conversation with her husband became more and more limited as they kept up a truce until the next time they were on holiday together.

It was the pleas for understanding from her children late one evening that brought reality back into her mind. She knew she had to show more overt love at home and more human sensitivity at work. Some deep conversations with her teenage children brought her back to reality at home. Some critical feedback at the office made her realize that she could not continue to ride roughshod over others.

She took conscious steps to reduce the level of discord, which she had begun to accept as normal. She felt she had made some limited progress but was conscious that the constraints on her life meant that she could not afford to become too soft-hearted.

In this chapter we look first at learning from discord, or creative friction, and at turning discord around and not wanting to be known as discordant. We then look at living with discord in your personal life and coping with realities that you would not wish on anybody else.

Learning from discord

Geoff was conscious that he did not get on as well with his boss as he had hoped. Their working relationship caused him huge frustration, but he recognized that he needed to work effectively with her. The steps he took were:

- To try to understand objectively the different perspectives they brought
- To see his boss regularly to understand her priorities
- To give his boss regular progress reports
- To be clear about the value-added he wanted from his boss and to agree the nature of that contribution with her
- To give her positive feedback about the contribution she was making in his area
- To watch if she irritated him and not to let his irritation show
- To summarize regularly to himself what he regarded as particularly positive in the approach that his boss brought

What he learned from the experience of working with his boss was:

- Not to assume that he and his boss would have the same priorities
- To recognize that every personality is different and that we each have our own preferences
- To accept that discord can sometimes be creative
- To be watchful of his body language so that his boss did not feel he was writing off her comments
- To retain the integrity of his approach and, while being aware of his boss's perspective, not to alter his own approach so radically that he undermined his effectiveness

The experience of working with his boss, although painful, taught him a set of new perspectives that would be valuable whatever role he went into. He was learning a lot from discord and was, reluctantly, happy to admit this.

Turning discord around

Richard had a difficult relationship with Margaret, one of his direct reports. When he had applied for his current role Margaret had also been a candidate for the post, and she had initially found it difficult to accept Richard as her boss. Richard recognized that a certain element of discord was inevitable. He kept his cool and was firm but never cross with Margaret. Over time they worked on a number of successful projects together. Margaret gradually settled down and accepted Richard as her boss, and she began to appreciate his approach.

The turning point was when Margaret was explicit about how much she was learning from him and expressed her gratitude to him. Richard breathed a sigh of relief. He had held his nerve and had kept working positively with his colleague. She was delighted with progress, as was Richard. He had turned discord around by building a long-term relationship.

Not wanting to be known as discordant

Terry liked to make progress through consensus. The words she was comfortable with people using about her were authoritative, active, engaged, persuasive, considered and responsible. The words that she did not want people to use about her were abrasive, impetuous or inconclusive. She reflected hard on the difference between being authoritative and being abrasive. She was determined to keep her cool, but one individual would continually test her patience. Terry did not want to be abrasive or aggressive, but quiet statements of authority did not seem to work. She knew that she had to hold certain people to account and press rather harder than perhaps she had done before. She had to stand her ground.

Terry's opportunity came when two interventions by the individual were misjudged. She had strong evidence to take action and was assertive in saying he needed to change his approach. Thankfully, he recognized the unfortunate effects of his interventions. He began gradually to change his approach. Terry had not wanted to be discordant but had reached the stage where she had to be direct. It worked, but only after she had concluded that a more direct approach was the only conceivable way forward. It was painful for her to accept the inevitability of this conclusion, but she was grateful that she had done so.

Sometimes it is right to be discordant. Those moments can be painful but hugely influential. Discordant moments are normally most effective when they are planned rather than when they just happen.

Allowing creative friction

It is friction between the tire and the road which creates the grip. Friction is not necessarily dangerous: it can be an essential part of staying on track. Moments of friction can be hugely creative and lead to a new perspective. Friction is not something to be feared, provided it is reasonably controlled.

Questions to ask yourself might be:

- What creative friction am I part of at the moment?
- What contribution can I make to ensure that the friction becomes more rather than less creative?
- Is fear of friction limiting the effectiveness of some exchanges?

Living with discord in your health

Patrick Chivers's left foot felt as though it was under assault from a thousand needles. His consultant told him that he had a mild form of Parkinson's disease. He was assured that the disease does not materially shorten your life, but he recognized that life would get tougher as he approached 60.

Questions flew through his mind about career, ambitions and finance. There were fears big and small. Alongside the pain he felt a strong sense of being blessed in many ways, blessed to have had good health for so long and thankful to be loved and to have a valued Christian faith.

Three months after Patrick had been told of the onset of the disease he wrote:

> I need to find peace in the face of this new foe. I still search for answers to the questions which press on me, especially in the watches of the night. And I have not quietened the fears which shout at me when I pause to let them.
>
> But I have come to understand that my struggle with this foe has the potential to define my life. Like it or not, I will be changed by the remorseless progress of the disease. I will, of course, stand my ground as I am able. Before this all broke over me I would have judged myself to be resilient and determined, the qualities needed for sustained rear guard action. But to focus all my energies on the slow, inevitable retreat would surely be a mistake.

I am now at one of those rare moments in life where I am open to profound change. Fleetingly, I have an opportunity to choose the nature of that change. The temptation is to ignore the opportunity and, instead, to hunker down for the long fight to come.

Am I thankful for having this opportunity? No, I cannot claim that – not for a moment. I am daunted by it, fearing it is as I fear the indignities and frustrations yet to come. I cannot muster gratitude, but I can see that if it had not been for the onset of ill health, I would not have know the giddy, intoxicating feeling of being borne aloft by my family and friends. For them I have only thanks. And I know that if it had not been for the disease, this would have been an Easter like any other – the choice before me hidden or ignored. I am a fortunate man, a hopeful man.

The onset of ill health can shake us profoundly. It can sometimes destroy us, but it can also reinforce our best qualities.

Living with discord in our health creates new tensions but means we rely on the personal resources that are most precious to us. The moment when the doctor gives us bad news can release new hopes about what is still doable and the relationships that continue to be important to us.

Living with harsh reality about our mortality

Eugene O'Kelly stepped into his doctor's office in May 2005 with a full calendar and a lifetime of plans on his mind. Six days later he would resign as CEO of KPMG. His lifetime of plans dwindled to 100 days. In his book, *Chasing Daylight: How My Forthcoming Death Transformed My Life*, Eugene talks of his last few months before he died of brain cancer.

In his book, which is haunting and yet hopeful, he reminds us to embrace the fragile, fleeting moments of our lives – the time we have with our family, our friends and even ourselves. He recalls sitting at the dining table making a to-do list for his final days to:

- Get legal and financial affairs in order
- "Unwind" relationships
- Simplify
- Live in the moment
- Create (but also be open to) great moments, "perfect" moments
- Begin transition to next state
- Plan funeral

He wanted his last period to be marked by resolution and closure, by heightened awareness, by the pleasure and joy of life. He wrote:

No more living in the future. (Or the past, for that matter – a problem for many people, although a lesser one for me.) I needed to stop living two months, one week, even a few hours ahead. Even a few minutes ahead. Sixty seconds from now is, in its way, as elusive as sixty years from now, and always will be. It is – was – exhausting to live in a world that never exists. Also kind of silly, since we happen to be blessed with such a fascinating one right here, right now.

I felt that if I could learn to stay in the present moment, to be fully conscious of my surroundings, I would buy myself lots of time that had never been available to me, not in all the years I was healthy. ... I would soon discover, though, that staying in the present and being genuinely conscious of my surroundings would be just about the hardest thing I had ever attempted.

He started to identify lots of people who did not live in the present, despite what they might have believed. The lived either in the future or in the past, or maybe nowhere at all. In particular, people who didn't listen, who asked questions without waiting for whole answers. People who were angry and bitter. People who could not distinguish between the forest and the trees.

He wrote:

Somehow, I had to learn how to be in the present moment, how to live there at least for snippets of time. ... In my mind, the future and the past fought until they had finally muscled out any chance of my experiencing something fresh and totally within my control – the present. ... Living in the present moment was tremendously difficult.

The final words that Eugene wrote in the book are about conversations with his mother and his brother:

I took my mother's hand and walked her to the front of the boat to talk, just the two of us. I told her I was in a good place. I told her I would see her in heaven. A person of deep faith, she was comfortable with that.

Later, my brother and I talked alone. He was angry – not at me but at life, that this should be happening to me. "Your anger won't do anyone any good," I told him. It would dissipate him, I said. He needed to try and live in the present. I told him to take the energy he was spending being angry at the world, double it, and channel it into love for his children. ... He promised me he would. I told my brother how proud I was of him. I told him what a great father I thought he was, and how great a dad he would continue to be.

It was a perfect day. I felt complete. Spent but complete.

This moving account by Eugene O'Kelly reminds us of the significance of living in the present moment. He had to live with the harsh reality of his impending death but continued to live in the moment for others. There was discord, which he coped with remarkably well, leaving moving memories of final conversations with so many.

Next steps

Moments of discord can be painful yet surprisingly enriching. They can be moments that shock us and shake us. Sometimes we have to sweat through them. On occasions there is a finality about discordant moments that is unavoidable. But perhaps discordant moments can have a more profound impact upon us than any other moments in our lives.

Questions to reflect on might be:

- When have I been able to turn discord around successfully?
- When has creative friction helped generate better outcomes?
- How afraid am I of being discordant?
- How best do I live with discords in my health?
- How prepared am I to live with the harsh reality of my mortality?

SECTION G

Creating future moments

Defining moments are not just about the past; they take us into the future. Using precious time effectively is central to our future wellbeing.

This section looks in turn at:

- Focus in the moment
- Rhythm of moments
- Creating moments for others

The section looks at making the best use of future moments by bringing a clear focus; it considers how shafts of stillness can help sharpen our focus on what is most important. It looks at creating a rhythm of moments that works best for us. Creating moments for others is about the tone we set and the way we enable those around us to find their own rhythms and grow in their leadership capabilities.

16 Focus in the moment

We need to be able both to focus in a particular moment and to escape that moment. We need to be able to give an issue our sole, undivided attention but not be so captured by it that we become insensitive to events happening around us. Effective focus is about blanking out irrelevant considerations, but it is also about moving our focus from one area to another, preferably with timing that we control. Focus is all about the quality of our attention.

Marilyn's story

Marilyn was always energetic. She could move from one subject to another quickly. She had an encyclopedic mind; she collected information and was always a valuable source of data.

Because of her eclectic mind colleagues began to use her more and more as a source of information. One consequence was that she became stretched sideways and at certain times did not get into the depth she needed to on particular issues.

On a few occasions she was caught out by the thinness of her knowledge. In the Planning Department where she worked she knew that her long-term future depended on her depth of understanding of issues. She recognized that she needed to bring a greater focus into her work and began to block out time to master the intricacies of new legal requirements. Her focus paid dividends, and she became trusted as an expert in this area.

The lesson for Marilyn was the importance of being clear what her areas of focus were going to be and building up a sharpness of credibility in those areas. Sometimes she had to hide herself away so that she was unavailable in order to give herself the time to focus on maintaining the depth of her expertise. The consequence was that the more that people sought her advice, the more assiduous she became in keeping herself up to speed on the latest developments.

Focusing in the moment involves being confident in the moment, stretching the moment and focusing on the benefit of the moment. But it is also about being aware if you become too focused in a moment and are unable to break out of it. Being fully equipped to focus in a moment involves creating shafts of stillness so that your focus is renewed.

Being confident in the moment

The more you are confident in the moment, the more focused you can be. Fiona talks of becoming increasingly confident at key moments:

> There is a defining moment when you are comfortable saying, "I am going to do it my way." It is being able to say, comfortably and confidently, "I know the right questions to ask." What gives confidence in focusing in the moment is the recognition that you have done difficult things and made them happen. Doing difficult things and seeing visible results is so encouraging. I did something and it worked! Looking back on difficult problems you have sorted gives you a great sense of accomplishment. It is an affirmation of your values when your approach works, e.g. when you delegate effectively to individuals and don't do it all yourself.

It is the firm acknowledgment of past successes that enables us to focus in the moment in a way that is confident and then gives confidence to others.

Stretching in the moment

When an individual is good at focusing in a moment the key question becomes how they can stretch the effectiveness of that moment. When Bernard and I discussed how he could stretch the effectiveness of his ability to focus in the moment he talked about the importance of clarifying in his own mind:

- Where he could add most value
- Which important issues he could he push forward
- Where he might rein back a bit
- What the pressure points were where he could provide even more leverage

An analogy can be made with a speaker who needs to get the attention of an audience. How does the speaker capture that interest and focus it even more? Once the audience's imagination has been caught, how can that interest be turned into action? The good preacher knows both how to catch the interest of the congregation and how to encourage some focused practical action. The most effective technique is not to tell your listeners precisely what they should focus on but to create a quality of engagement which means that listeners take the thoughts they are hearing and turn them into their own clarity of focus and action. Helping individuals to stretch their focus is rarely about telling them precisely what to do. It is more often about enabling them to take their own insights to the next stage.

Nicolas had become increasingly effective as a chair of meetings, but he knew he needed to stretch his abilities even further. He committed himself to:

- Observe how people were responding to his chairing
- Experiment with different techniques and skills
- Write notes after each meeting to self-assess his contribution
- Seek informal feedback from those attending the meeting
- Believe that he had good chairing skills and could be more confident in chairing meetings
- Keep using questions in a powerful way
- Be conscious of how he was using humor as a technique in his chairing

However good we might be at focusing in a moment, we should ask ourselves how we can take that skill to the next level. A good chairperson can always become more effective. Chairing is not about a single-minded focus on getting your personal conclusions agreed. It is about focusing on what is most important for the organization or the participants so that the end result is a set of outcomes consistent with what the committee is there to do. Often things are not that straightforward.

Preparing for an interview

Preparing for an interview is an example of focusing on a particular moment. Effective preparation is not just about the collection of information; it is about a clear focus on what you want to communicate in the interview. Effective preparation involves:

- Spending time sitting in the role you are applying for so that you understand the nature of the job and the type of pressures you would be under

- Thinking through clearly the decisions you would make in the role
- Imagining yourself leading the team and speaking to the media about the work of your organization
- Being clear what you would enjoy about the job and what would uplift you
- Viewing those interviewing you as colleagues you would enjoy working with

Effective preparation for an interview is not about:

- Rolling out a huge amount of detail
- Solving every problem that the organization faces
- Believing you can revolutionize the organization on day one
- Believing that you can achieve the transformation single-handedly

Effective focus in preparing for an interview is about:

- Thinking through the key issues
- Being clear on the type of leadership you would bring
- Having some clarity about the outcomes you would want to see achieved
- Being clear how you would lead and motivate others
- Bringing a balance between purposefulness and realism

The paradox is that for you to be fully focused in an interview, some of the best preparation can be to un-focus your mind. Prerequisites before the interview are good, relaxing sleep, some physical activity such as running or swimming, some good conversation about entirely different subjects and emptying of your mind of clutter.

Focusing on the benefits of particular moments

Vicky had been used to a world where she was influential and was able to generate a lot of change. She was now in more of an advisory role, which gave her fewer direct levers. This was initially a source of frustration to her. But her subsequent profound learning was about:

- The importance of influencing people without having hands-on power
- Recognizing that you cannot win a war every day

- Recognizing that ideas sometimes have their right time
- The importance of having a clear line of sight when an opportunity arises
- Sometimes having to live with "stuckness"
- Recognizing the reality that action needs to take place on a number of fronts but being ready to take opportunities and openings when they arise

Vicky felt uneasy about this new role initially, but she came to feel that she could focus more on the most effective ways of ensuring progress. She had the confidence to use a wider range of approaches, be a bit more subtle, work through the problems she was trying to solve carefully in order to reach the outcomes she wanted.

Looking at future focus

At a point of transition or a particular milestone it can be helpful to re-evaluate what your future focus should be. When Bob, a senior leader within the UK government, was looking at the impending impact of tighter resources he was clear that the elements that would be most important included:

- Ensuring there was a sense of going forward even if resources were tight
- Building a clear narrative to take people with you
- Ensuring sound intelligence in order to do necessary things well
- Working across boundaries effectively

Bob saw leading change effectively at a time of tight resources as being about:

- Coping with less money and using available resources well
- Responding to the continuous pressure for quality and to increasing expectations
- Recognizing the necessity of more citizen empowerment
- Seizing technological change and using it to best effect
- Inspiring a more complex workforce
- Identifying key pathways through which progress could be made
- Responding well to unexpected shocks
- Coping with destabilizing issues

Asking ourselves periodically about the future focus for our work and leadership is essential. We might find it best to do this exercise alone, with trusted colleagues or with an external mentor or coach. Different approaches work for different people. Leaders who can set out the focus clearly will take their people with them. If the focus is lost in a blur of words the motivation of the audience will dissipate.

Being too focused in the moment

Sometimes there is a risk of being too focused in the moment. We are enthused by colleagues and leave a meeting intent on making a big difference. But realism might not have been part of the discussion, and the enthusiasm soon wanes. Any discussion with a focus on outcomes needs to involve some consideration of risks and threats; otherwise the outcomes will not be securely based.

The BlackBerry is useful in providing a quick means of communicating by e-mail or text, but it can be a distraction and take us away from key priorities. One Chief Executive banned his staff from looking at their Black-Berry during meetings. In one sense looking at the diary on a BlackBerry is no more harmful than looking at a paper diary in a sheaf of papers. But the irritation caused by looking at a BlackBerry was such that the only way to ensure full attention was to ban them from being used in meetings.

The art of using a BlackBerry or texting well is boxing the time when it is used; it involves a five-minute focus on the device when traveling between meetings and then moving the focus away from the BlackBerry and on to the next discussion. Being able to give your undivided attention and then switch that attention from one thing to another without diluting the focus on each individual item is a precious skill.

Creating shafts of stillness

Creating shafts of stillness can be one of the most powerful contributors to our being able to focus in the moment well. We tend to contrast activity and stillness and to put them into different boxes. Activity is for the working day, and stillness might get a look-in at the weekend. A shaft of light can bring a new perspective to a dark scene. A shaft of stillness might bring a new perspective to a busy day.

The word "shaft" suggests something that is deep and straight-sided. A shaft of light can penetrate long distances. A shaft of stillness can be deep and strong in enabling us to keep a busy day in perspective.

On a practical level a shaft of stillness might involve walking slowly between meetings, going out to buy a cup of coffee, breathing more deeply, allowing your brain to turn off for five minutes, walking around the block at lunchtime, looking at a favorite picture, smiling at a good memory or glancing through the newspaper headlines.

Shafts of stillness are more about an attitude of mind than a set of actions. A sense of stillness in our work can come from understanding where we can add most value, accepting our own strengths and limitations, recognizing the financial and political restrictions on what we can do, having a reasonably settled view about priorities with colleagues and accepting what is and is not possible.

Stillness does not come from ignoring reality or 'hiding your light under a bushel'. It enables you to face up to reality, to recognize its significance and to focus your drive and energy where they can have most effect. Shafts of stillness are very personal: what works for you might not work for others. The stillness might not be a solitary act. Five minutes' fresh air with a good colleague can result in both stillness and new energy.

The biggest detriment to stillness is relentless noise in our heads. There are different voices saying that we must try harder; we must fill every moment of the day; we must remember X, Y and Z; we must be seen to be active; we must succeed every day; we must deliver.

Can we sometimes say to these voices, "Thank you. I hear what you are saying." Can we then park some of these voices and ask ourselves:

- What is the most important task on my agenda?
- Can I chunk up my time and energy?
- What is the best order in which to tackle what is before me?
- How can I create variety and interest in my working day?
- When am I going to allow myself to smile?

Maybe stillness is about creating other voices in our head. Mantras such as "You can only do what you can do" can help create a rhythm in our breathing and in our thoughts.

When there is hyperactivity all around us, can we allow ourselves to take a five-minute time-out? Smokers are required to take time out away from others. Perhaps the rest of us could sometimes adopt the same practice of a five-minute break; we would then return fresh. Before I see a coaching client I try to have five minutes of stillness reflecting on how the individual is likely to be feeling as they walk into the office. Five minutes of reflective stillness thinking about my client is worth more than 30 minutes of intense preparation.

If stillness for you is about walking through a forest, walking on a beach or the silence after a youngster falls asleep, can you recreate some of the same sensations as you picture the scene or the emotions? The intense activity in many jobs makes the search for shafts of stillness even more important. The relentless pressure to do more with less means the discontinuity between ambition and reality will widen.

Essential to thriving and surviving and being able to keep a clear focus on what is most important will be creating shafts of stillness. The gentle plant needs a shaft of light to survive and grow. We mere mortals need shafts of stillness to survive, grow and flourish.

Questions to ask ourselves might be:

- What are the shafts of stillness that are most important to me?
- How can I generate more shafts of stillness to enable me to focus even more effectively on my priorities?
- How can I build even more shafts of stillness into my life?

Next steps

Next steps might involve practicing the art of being focused in the moment. Providing the best quality of listening and engagement is both a precious gift to others and an expression of our concern to use time and energy well. Striking the right balance between activity on the Black-Berry and moments of stillness might seem elusive but is so precious.

Questions to reflect on might be:

- When am I most focused in the moment?
- How can I use my ability to focus in the moment to prepare effectively for future meetings or interviews?
- How can I stretch my focus in some situations even more, to have the impact I want?
- Can I bring a future focus to bear on a regular basis by working through future events in my mind?
- How can I use shafts of stillness to even more powerful effect to enable me to be refreshed and to focus more effectively?

17 Rhythm of moments

Most people who are reasonably successful and happy in their work have a rhythm in their use of time and energy which works well for them. The rhythm is not inviolate – sometimes it has to change – but there is a regular return to the pattern of the rhythm whenever possible. If the rhythm is broken for too long there can be discord and a sense of being out of control. Knowing and enjoying the rhythm of moments that works best for us is a key part of how we survive and thrive.

Sandra's story

Sandra prided herself on ordering her day in a way which kept her in reasonable equilibrium. She organized her diary around key meetings and was always willing to say "no" if she judged their priority not to be high enough. Her boss was concerned that these rhythms were, on some occasions, about Sandra's priorities not his. He could feel a growing resentment in himself and knew that he had to tackle this before it festered any more. He was frank with Sandra about the way she prioritized. Sandra recognized that she needed to make some movement in her boss's direction but used the discussion as a perfectly sensible negotiation to arrive at shared priorities. The discussion enabled her to be explicit about how she wanted to allocate some inviolate time for long-term thinking and planning.

Sandra knew that the equilibrium she had agreed with her boss would not last for ever, but there were some fixed points in their understanding which meant she could maintain a rhythm in her use of time and energy and could get home at a reasonable hour. She had established a relationship with her boss in which they could talk frankly about maintaining a rhythm of working that was effective for both of them.

This chapter looks at different aspects of a rhythm of moments, such as changing habits, recognizing when you have choices, going with the flow, choosing the right moment and getting on the front foot. It also addresses how to create rhythms for the day and term that work best for you. (As I worked in the UK government Department for Education for many years, the natural split of the year for me is into three terms: summer to Christmas, Christmas to Easter, and Easter to summer.)

Changing habits

Many of our rhythms are firmly embedded. Many people consistently drive their car at 38 mph in urban areas rather than 30 mph; they do this automatically, as habitual practice. When Wendy was caught by a speeding camera she went on a course to avoid having points put on her license. One theme from the course was that speeding is about habit, with retraining taking 21 days! The course was about creating new patterns so that traveling at 30 mph rather 38 mph becomes normal: the instructors suggested that only after doing it for 21 days does traveling at 30 mph become the automatic behavior response. Wendy's conclusion was that changing habits is really hard!

Establishing good habits seems self-righteous. Removing bad habits has a flavor of being a naughty child. But our lives are full of habits – of habitual behavior which we do automatically. Creating good habits in our use of time and energy is a fundamental requirement in creating a good rhythm. At a basic level it might be helpful to ask yourself:

- What are my good habits that I would like to embed further?
- What other good habits would I like to develop?
- What are the bad habits I would like to remove?

The importance of persistent challenge

In three successive Director General jobs I recruited one individual to work for me as a Deputy Director in each role. She was an impressive leader and was superb at upwardly managing me. She would always be direct with me, and I knew I could trust her totally because her judgment was consistently sound. Her persistent challenge was important to me.

Helen talks of one person who worked for her in three different places. He would always hassle her – telling her off for running into her office. He was persistent in saying to Helen that she should talk to her people more and give them more time. He was clear that Helen needed to be seen to spend time with her staff at least once a day. He still presses Helen, who recognizes that she takes some, but not enough, account of his perspective. Without his persistent comments she would never stop running from meeting to meeting.

Recognizing when you have choices

Often we have no choice. For example, at the start of the academic year a teacher does not have the option of applying for a new job. If there is a down-turn in the market and there are no new jobs available in your engineering company, there are no realistic opportunities to move to another company. If you are part-way through your training, you recognize that it would be folly to move somewhere else before you are fully qualified.

But sometimes there are choices. For example:

■ Your project is coming to an end.
■ The organization is about to expand or contract.
■ The market is changing and there are new opportunities.

Recognizing that you have choices is about both an accurate perception of whether opportunities exist and your willingness to change your current pattern of life to respond to those opportunities. Believing that you have choices is not just about day-dreaming. It is about a willingness to break a current pattern or cycle. It is about being willing to take risks and do what you have often wanted, but have been reluctant, to do.

Olivier had been in her current role for 18 months. Her choice was either to stay in the role and make an even bigger impact or to seek to move on to a different position. She was balancing personal preferences, career aspirations and the needs of the organization. Eventually the needs of the organization meant that she was strongly encouraged to move into a demanding leadership role. The process of weighing up the option of staying or moving had helped her be clear about what in her current rhythm was positive and what had become boring and possibly stultifying.

It might be worth asking yourself:

■ How effectively do I frame different choices so that I look at them as objectively as possible?
■ What types of choice am I facing at the moment, and how well am I handling them?
■ Are there moments of choice for me which I do not fully recognize?

It was a life-changing moment for Norman when he recognized that there were genuine moments of choice in his life: every day there were moments of choice about his attitude. A defining moment can be when we change our attitude toward individuals or issues and break the current constraining rhythm in our mind.

Recognizing when you are on a roll

There are moments when you can do no wrong and other moments when it appears you can do no right. When you are on a roll do not be embarrassed about it. There will be times when people respond positively to your leadership. It is a case of going with the flow at these moments.

On other occasions everything you suggest is dismissed. Your views seem to be the wrong views, at the wrong time on the wrong subject. When that happens the choice can be as stark as either moving on or adapting some of your perspectives to meet the expectations of the people you are working with.

Sometimes you might continue to take an unpopular view because you believe that expectations will change, that the force of circumstances means that your perspective will eventually be re-accepted. But it is not always possible to hang on. Sometimes it is necessary to decide consciously and emotionally that it is time to get off the bus.

Getting on the front foot

When Deidre was getting herself established in a big leadership role she recognized that reviewing progress at the end of the day or week did not work for her. The best approach for her was asking questions in the moment, such as:

- How would I feel if someone said to me now that I was being indecisive?
- What would being decisive in the moment mean?

What helped her move forward and be willing to get on the front foot was:

- Being comfortable and assertive at the same time
- Recognizing that she needed to stay intellectually sharp
- Tutoring herself to stand back in the moment so that she consciously recognized what she was thinking about and what she was worrying about

■ Building in time to reflect as she recognized that she was, by inclination, an activist

Deirdre knew that her best ideas came to her when she was out walking in the fresh air; hence it was important to build in plenty of opportunities for walking briskly at lunchtime and at the weekend.

When you are at the end of your driveway in your car waiting to pull out into the main road, there is a right moment to choose to move into the stream of traffic. You are recognizing the pattern of the movement of the cars and not trying to distort that rhythm. You want to join the traffic smoothly, when there is space for you. Getting on the front foot is about seeing opportunities and moving into the space. Sometimes it is about creating your own space, but not in a self-destructive way.

Rediscovering rhythms

Andrea, who grew up in a small town, enjoyed university life, building a career and getting married. In her late 40s her marriage came to an end, although the two of them remained friends. In one sense the end of the marriage was tragic, but Andrea rediscovered herself and built a new life. There was a sense of liberation which enabled her to follow up various cultural interests and make new friendships.

The rhythm of her life had been fine for 25 years, but in retrospect she felt it had been a bit flat. She was rejuvenated, had grown hugely in confidence and was willing to stretch the boundaries of her own thinking, make new friendships and explore new avenues. It was an exciting time as she rediscovered herself and created a new rhythm of moments that worked well for her.

Creating rhythms for the day or the term that work well for you

Gordon recognized that some of his rhythms had got out of control. He was working excessively long hours and not getting enough sleep or exercise. He was ending up feeling grumpy both at work and at home. He recognized that some action was necessary.

He was clear that he wanted to build a better rhythm into his use of time during the day and during each term. Within each day there needed to be time for meetings, reading papers, doing e-mail, preparing and thinking. He divided the year into three terms, and at the start of each term he would take time to review action that had happened in the previous three or four months and his priorities for the next three or four months.

Crucial to success for Gordon was a personal assistant who organized the use of his time and a coach who held him to account. The right geographical space was also important to him: some of his thinking space was either at home, out walking or in the library. Once or twice a year he would give himself the opportunity to go away for a day to think through key priorities for the next phase. He brought a rigorous discipline to creating the right rhythms for the day and the term. Often the events of the week swept some of those disciplines aside, but he always aimed to return to his rhythms as quickly as possible. This approach enabled him to keep going effectively as a senior leader well into his late 60s.

Questions to ask yourself might be:

- Are there recognizable rhythms in my day or term?
- Are there patterns I want to reinforce?
- What would make the biggest difference in terms of helping embed good habits within the rhythm?

Creating private space

There is an important theme for many people about creating quiet moments. It is crucial to be alert to the danger of our time getting completely filled up. David Bell, the Permanent Secretary at the Department for Education in London, talks of practices that have been useful to him. There is a space he uses in the Cabinet Office on a Wednesday morning, before the regular Permanent Secretaries' meeting, where he will go and sit and reflect on the week so far and write down summary notes. For a couple of years, when he was on holiday in Portugal, he wrote papers about what he was observing in terms of the work of the department and what the next steps might be. He comments:

> It is important to create moments where there is time and space. It is about you personally regenerating. It is topping up the fuel tank. Creating a rhythm of moments is important. I try to be protective of large parts of the weekend. When there are crisis moments your rhythm is disrupted but even in a crisis it is important to create space and a new rhythm of moments.

David talks about the importance of translation moments which follow reflection. He says of himself:

> I am not primarily a creative, imaginative thinker. What I do seem to be good at is assimilating, reconfiguring and translating into what should happen next. I can reasonably quickly understand what we need to do and get to translation moments.

David recognizes that he has a tendency to be decisive, and, therefore, he has built into his rhythm time to reflect on his own.

Many leaders talk about the importance of creating quiet moments within whatever is the rhythm of their day. Moments of aloneness are to be treasured as they enable us to put what is being loaded upon us into a wider context.

Moments of looking forward

A rhythm that is stuck in the past or even in the present can be exhausting after a while. For most of us it is important to have a rhythm that takes us into the future and to have a few things to look forward to that keep our spirits up, even on the most demanding of days. It might be looking forward to what is going to happen next weekend or our next holiday or a future conversation with a friend.

Moments of looking forward need not be about wishful thinking. They can be about recognizing current reality but also maintaining a sense of positive movement and hope. Very few things stand still; they go either backward or forward. Moments of looking forward keep us fresh and cheerful, provided they do not destabilize a fragile current equilibrium.

Recognizing your own cycles

Many of us have our own patterns of emotional experiences, for example, when we start a new role. Rowena comments:

> I often arrive in a job and find myself hating it and longing for what I used to be doing. I then recognize the patterns. As soon as I have set up networks and feel established in the job I start to feel comfortable. Initially I do not want to lose face. Being an expert overnight is a problem and, in the first 6 months, I do not feel that comfortable.

After 9 to 12 months I feel comfortable. After 2 years I feel very comfortable but after 2 to 3 years I can get bored!

Recognizing and understanding our own cycle of emotional reactions and seeing the pattern can provide reassurance even when the going is tough. Knowing that we always go through a particular cycle can make such a difference in our acceptance of the inevitability of some down moments in our normal rhythm.

Creating new rhythms

Whatever our rhythm of moments, we can vary it. Charlie talks about the life-changing effect of working on his allotment, where he treats time very differently. It helped him create a new rhythm. Charlie comments:

Rather than running from one thing to another, as I do in the workplace, work in the allotment is something I find therapeutic because I can't do it in a rush – several hours will go past without you noticing, and so there is an almost timeless quality to it. And because it is work that requires little direct thought or decision-making, it creates time and space for reflection that both puts things into perspective and brings new perspectives.

Working on his allotment has brought home to Charlie the importance of different rhythms of life. He now views time in a different way, and he is now much more conscious about how non-work activities feed into his work and his wider equilibrium.

Next steps

We do have choices; we are never completely captive to our current situation. What holds us back from progress is normally ourselves. Moving on requires that precious combination of enjoying the rhythms that work best for us and continually embracing new rhythms that help give us energy and renewal. It can be helpful to take stock of the rhythms that you are operating to. This can involve writing them down or talking them through with a friend. One approach is to identify:

- Three aspects of your rhythm which are very precious and important
- Three aspects of your rhythm which you might wish to change

■ New elements you would like to build into the rhythm of your life

Questions to ask yourself might be:

■ How much do I recognize that there is a rhythm of moments that governs my life?
■ How well do I cope if that rhythm is challenged?
■ How able am I to choose the right moment to change the rhythm?
■ Is there scope for me to reassess what rhythms might work best for me in the future?
■ How open am I to radically different rhythms?

18 Creating moments for others

Creating good moments for others can be a source of encouragement and fulfillment. Moments when we see people grow and take opportunities that they have long resisted can be a delight. Creating moments for others is never about telling them what to do: it is about creating a situation in which they can experience new or different moments that have a powerful effect on them. This might involve protecting somebody for a while to give them time to reflect; on other occasions it might involve asking incisive questions that help them work through to next steps.

Gemma's story

Gemma had reached a stage in her career where there was a bit of space in her diary. She had built an excellent team and delegated wisely to them. She took as her guiding principle that she should do only those things which only she could do. Everything else ought to be delegated.

One consequence was that she developed some thinking space. Part of it she used for pushing the boundaries on long-term developments. She became increasingly interested in how best to develop and grow her people. She spent quality time mentoring both her direct reports and others with potential within her organization. The mentoring gave her huge satisfaction.

Her delight in her job now was not just the excellent results that her organization produced but also the step-change she saw in some of her people as they responded well to her mentoring and took on ever-greater levels of responsibility. She wanted to build a group of strong candidates who could potentially succeed her, even though in the medium term this might make her own position more vulnerable.

Creating moments for others is about creating a context where people can grow, where there can be effective engagement, where there can be healing and where people can move on and leave behind difficult or unhappy phases of their lives.

Creating moments when people can grow

The action of a leader often becomes a defining moment for other people. The leader who launches a new product creates a whole set of opportunities for their staff at each stage in the development, production and marketing of the product. Individuals will either be confident enough to take those opportunities or shrink from them. In launching a product the leader is creating the opportunity for different moments that can be significant for many people in the organization.

An individual leader might have limited understanding of the long-term consequences of some actions. The government minister launching a new scheme can create important moments for thousands of people in different parts of the country as they bid for funds and seek to use those funds effectively. Even a family decision to build a house extension creates opportunities and potentially important moments for the builders and those with specialist skills working on the extension. All of our actions create consequences in terms of generating important moments for others.

When an important task has to be done, often our first inclination is to do it ourselves. That way we ensure that the outcome is right and that we get appropriate credit! But giving ourselves a good moment can mean denying that moment to somebody else. Maybe another individual would not approach the task in the same way we would; perhaps the outcome would not be quite as polished, but it might still be fit for purpose. Passing a task to someone else can provide them with an opportunity to experiment, widen their repertoire and develop their self-confidence.

Kathryn was grateful to her boss for helping her grow her confidence by participating in cross-departmental meetings. Her boss had taken her with him on a couple of occasions, and she had begun to get the measure of which types of contribution were most effective. Then her boss asked Kathryn to go on her own to some of these meetings. Kathryn was apprehensive at first, and she said nothing at the first meeting. Gradually she became more confident and began to express her perspective. Over time she developed sharper focus in the timing of her interventions and became increasingly influential. Kathryn was for ever grateful to her boss for inducting her into the meetings, giving her sound advice and then letting her take the lead, develop her approach and grow her own distinctive personal contribution and impact.

It might be worth reflecting on:

- Who has created moments for me that I have been able to use well?
- What was their balance between steering me and setting me free?
- How often do I mirror the approach of these role models?

Creating healing moments for others

Matt Baggott, the Chief Constable of the Police Service of Northern Ireland, talks of the importance of the healing role as a senior police officer. His perspective is:

> Healing involves both providing clear expectations of our value-added to people's lives and creating opportunities to say thank you when these are fulfilled. It is often how you put people back together who deal with difficulty and complexity and become jaded. Healing includes recognition of personal worth and contribution. The ceremony of giving medals and commendations is very important, linked with speeches which acknowledge the efforts and sacrifices of the recipients.
>
> Likewise in terms of neighborhood policing the healing role is important. You are the honest broker in communities. Justice itself can be a healing process. The question is how do you do the restorative bit? When there has been a crime, justice needs to be seen to be done, which helps provide healing for the victim. Acknowledging wrong and healing can go together, although justice must always be proportionate to the seriousness of the crime. It can be cathartic. Healing is about enabling individuals and communities to move on.
>
> We have to give people the opportunity to be reflective of their role and influence beyond simply following procedures. We also need to allow justice and healing to be seen together.

The external view of police officers is that they are there to bring justice. But perhaps even more important is the healing they can bring through their influence in communities and their interaction with both victim and aggressor.

If a senior police officer can have an effective role in creating healing moments, perhaps the rest of us can see our potential for bringing healing. In any organization there will be bruised people feeling resentment and unfairness, people who feel battered by external pressures and hard done by. We might recognize in the organization in which we work:

- Individuals who have missed out on promotion
- Groups who have been facing severe criticism
- Groups who have produced a lot of work without much feeling of appreciation
- Managers who have had to deal with sharply conflicting priorities

■ Individuals whose status has been reduced through no fault of their own but as a consequence of external market changes

Any organization includes people who need healing. Sometimes they need to heal themselves. The most effective source of healing may be outside the organization: their families and friendships. But there is a responsibility on individual leaders in an organization to be aware when healing is needed and sometimes to be willing to be an agent of healing, or at least a facilitator of it. Sometimes healing might be about:

■ Allowing an individual to let off steam
■ Encouraging two people to talk through their different perspectives
■ Asking questions openly but insistently to enable someone to reflect on how they might heal themselves
■ Providing an atmosphere of support within a team or organization so that a healing process can take place
■ Acknowledging to yourself when you have moved into a new place in which some of the previous resentment has been sidelined

Creating moments of engagement with others

Creating moments for others often involves acting as an agent through dialogue or questions that enable the other person to work out their own next steps. Creating effective engagement is important to give someone the confidence and the sense of freedom to articulate their own ideas and become more confident about them.

In our book *Business Coaching: Achieving Practical Results though Effective Engagement*, Robin Linnecar and I talked about the "golden thread" running through effective engagement. The elements in the golden thread are that the engagement is:

■ *Respectful*: bringing trust and unconditional mutual regard
■ *Listening*: being fully present and giving someone our sole, undivided attention
■ *Open-minded*: banishing preconceived notions, being fully on the other person's agenda and finding the point of need
■ *Flexible*: varying the approach, pace and timing to fit the circumstances of the individual
■ *Supportive*: bringing encouragement, emphasizing the positive and helping individuals keep up their energy

- *Challenging*: involving quality engagement between equals slicing through the 'dross'
- *Forward-looking*: bringing a relentless focus on the future, whatever past or current travails there are

The more we can engage effectively with others, the more we create moments for them to stretch and develop their own thinking. One of the joys of doing executive coaching or mentoring is the opportunity you are able to give people to stretch their own thinking. The more we can adopt a coaching approach in whatever line of work we are in, the more we can help people grow in confidence and effectiveness.

Learning from moments that did not work quite as we wanted

Marilyn tells a story about a career crisis that led to a new and different avenue. Marilyn was a qualified accountant and had been a Group Financial Controller. She was given the opportunity to become the Managing Director of a small subsidiary, which she was very excited about and saw as an important career step. Her focus was getting a new IT system in place, but increasingly she felt 'stuck in the middle'. There had been the initial excitement of becoming Managing Director, but the job involved a long commute and sapped her energy. She also had to deal with the pressure of making people redundant, a new experience for her. She suddenly thought, "I'm not enjoying it; I am not myself. I know I am close to breaking down. I would rather be unemployed than doing this."

When she left the organization she did some consultancy work initially and then went to work at a professional accountancy body. Marilyn had her life back and was doing something she enjoyed. When she had moved on from her Managing Director role there had been a sense of relief linked with a sense of bereavement. The experience had left her with the understanding that nobody is indispensable.

Marilyn had moved on, and she took a lot of learning with her. She drew from her experience in conversations with many other people. The difficult experience had not been wasted as it had given her a sense of what type of resilience was important to keep her going and of when she needed to switch direction.

Sometimes we can think that the times when we "fail" are to be forgotten or ignored. But apparent failures often give us our richest experiences. In my coaching work I draw far more from my failures than from my successes. I hope in a small way that sharing my own experiences creates moments for others to reflect on what has worked well for them.

Next steps

We might have more chances to create opportunities for others than we realize. When we have five-minute conversations with people we are either uplifting them or depressing them. Words of encouragement or quiet reflection can stimulate new energy in individuals. On other occasions creating moments for others is about giving them lots of space either to talk or to be on their own.

Questions to reflect on might be:

- Whom do I particularly treasure who has created moments for me?
- In my current use of time and energy whom do I create moments for?
- What sort of healing moments can I create for others?
- Through the way I engage with others how can I help them grow and stretch themselves?
- What are a couple of practical steps I can take to create moments that matter for people who are important to me?

Section H

The way forward

Moments do not happen in isolation. It is helpful to try to see the pattern and the linkages as we look both backward and to the future.

This concluding section looks at:

- Seeing the pattern of moments
- Next steps

I hope that it will provide a source of reflection and encouragement as you move on to the next defining moments in your life.

19 Seeing the pattern of moments

Individual defining moments are significant in themselves, but it is worth looking at the relationships between different defining moments. Are there interdependencies? Does one sort of defining moment tend to lead to another type of moment? Is there a pattern which it is helpful to recognize? Is there sometimes a spiral downward or a spiral upward?

The year 2009 was special for Frances and me as it was full of good moments. Our elder son, Graham, got married to Anna, and our daughter, Ruth, got married to Owen. Both these marriages were superb celebrations. Frances and I both reached the age of 60 in 2009 and had celebrations with friends in Guildford and Yorkshire. We went to New Zealand for Frances' 60th birthday and walked the Yorkshire Wolds Way for my 60th. Each event was delightful in its own right, but it was the linking of them together in a special year which was particularly memorable.

In contrast, in the late 1990s my mother, brother and uncle died within a few months of each other. These were three very sad events, and the grieving process was longer and deeper than I had expected.

In a bizarre way good events or painful events often happen in threes. Perhaps we are looking for this pattern, or perhaps when we have good moments we are more open to good moments and when there are sad moments we feel the sadness in other events even more.

Perhaps there are phases in our lives when a lot of defining moments happen quite close together. In other phases, life can be quite dull or unchanging for a relatively long period.

When defining moments come thick and fast we might long for a period of calm, but when life is a bit straightforward we might well seek a significant moment that changes our thinking or perspective.

Patterns of moments

It can be helpful to look back and see what the pattern of defining moments has been. Which ones have been linked? What was the catalyst that sparked off a particular sequence of defining moments? When has a painful or difficult moment released in you new understanding, with the consequence that you have become more receptive to moments of new insight.

On the other hand, have there been times when one difficult moment set off a downward spiral and you became somewhat defensive and closed down? What helped break a pattern in which the spiral was downward? Perhaps it was the chance of a day away, the support of family and friends or the opening up of new opportunities, or perhaps it was just plain straightforward dogged persistence.

Present patterns

Our personal survival can depend on our being able to focus on one priority at a time. I am appalling at multitasking! Giving a task our sole, undivided attention is probably the best way of ensuring we deliver the change we want, but understanding the links between different difficulties, pressures and emotions is important.

In each month there will be a cacophony of moments. Is it helpful to look at the linkages? When has one tricky moment led to another? When has one good outcome led to other positive moments?

Recognizing the effect that different types of moments have on our energy levels will enable us either to refresh and renew our energy or to recognize that it is being sapped even more.

Perhaps our lives are like a tapestry; maybe there is more of a pattern than we first realize. The pattern might flow from our cultural or personal backgrounds and our preferences or predilections. It might flow from the friends we keep and the way we spend our time. As the tapestry grows we can influence whether it has a coarse weave or a fine mesh.

Future patterns

Life does not end at 40 or 60 or 80. Some say that 60 is the new 40, and 80 is the new 60! If we see our defining moments purely as parts of our past, there is a risk that we will spend our time in the past. If we see our lives as a journey of defining moments that will continue well into the future, we can expect continued growth in our understanding and wisdom.

As we look ahead some defining moments will happen whether we like it or not. Other defining moments we can create. The death of a friend is a painful moment we do not seek. The experience of spending some time in a third world country can be a defining moment which shapes and molds our understanding in new ways.

As you look forward I encourage you to search for patterns and interdependencies. As we link enjoyable moments with ones that are more painful, there is a wholeness and richness about our life experience that enables us to appreciate what we are rooted in and what is most important about our next steps.

Key questions to ask yourself might be:

- When has one defining moment led to a sequence of other defining moments?
- Has there sometimes been a pattern of threes of either good moments or difficult moments? Has it been helpful to see it as a pattern?
- What has helped change a downward spiral of moments into an upward spiral?
- What future pattern of moments am I looking for?
- Am I able to be both purposeful and relaxed as I look forward to whatever is the future tapestry of defining moments?

20 Next steps

Defining moments is a theme that resonates with many people. What stories about defining moments have you heard in the past few weeks? Perhaps the stories below echo some of those you have listened to.

Jeff's story

Jeff had had a difficult bout of pneumonia, and his energy had been sapped. He gradually reached a point where he could go out of the house for one activity a day, which forced him to be much more self-disciplined than he had ever been before. He weighed up whether, on a particular day, he should go to church, drop in on a 60th birthday party, go out for a walk with his teenage son or clear some of the snow from the garden path. He wanted to do all four things; normally he would have done all four and more. He made a sort of compromise, going for a short walk with his son and dropping in on the 60th birthday celebration of his friend. He paid his son some pocket money to do some of the snow clearing and, on this occasion, read some of the psalms rather than going to church.

For Jeff the long tail of the effect of pneumonia made him more conscious of his use of time and energy than ever before. From then on he became much more selective. For Jeff having pneumonia had been a defining moment. He thought he would never properly recover, but gradually he did so. Church, friends, family and physical exercise all had their part, but perhaps in a more focused way than before. The main change was that his ambition at work for promotion was diminished but his ambition to spend time with family and friends was increased.

Bob's story

Bob is in his late 40s and revels in his work as a teacher in a junior school. His wife is Managing Partner of a professional services practice. Bob talks of two key defining moments that affected his career. The first was when he and his wife decided after their first youngster was born that Bob would stay at home and his wife would return full time to work. For 15 years he was very happily a house husband. The second defining moment came when he was spending some time doing voluntary teaching assistant work in an infants school and the head teacher said, "You would be a really good teacher." This positive comment caught his imagination; he trained as a teacher and is now loving it.

The two defining moments for Bob were a helpful conversation with his wife in which they agreed about the best use of their respective time and energy, and then the wonderful words of encouragement from an infant school head teacher about Bob having the potential to be an excellent teacher. There was no knowing at the time the first of these defining moments took place that it would lead to the second, but without the first defining moment the second would not have happened.

Jim's story

Jim had never been particularly happy at school and had not enjoyed the same academic success as his friends and siblings. He possessed practical skills and did a sequence of carpentry courses, but it all rather petered out and he eventually did clerical work, which he quite enjoyed but without being fulfilled.

What Jim had missed out on was a defining moment when somebody recognized his carpentry skills and began to mentor him. If someone had metaphorically put their arm around him and said, "You can do it," then perhaps he would have become a skilled carpenter, able to live off the proceeds of his work, but, sadly, that was not to be.

Risks to avoid

Risks involve missing an opportunity or interpreting it wrongly. Missing an opportunity might be a consequence of:

- Not preparing effectively
- Assuming a situation is worse than it is
- Feeling you are stuck
- Not taking responsibility for your actions
- Not feeling you have the energy to make a difference

Risks in interpreting a situation wrongly might include:

- Letting your emotions get in the way
- Over-reacting to an opportunity

- Trying too hard
- Believing only immediate action is worthwhile
- Thinking that you are the only person who can solve a particular problem

Central to avoiding these risks is a combination of self-awareness and good feedback. Self-awareness is about understanding your own strengths and foibles and your reactions to particular situations. Good-quality feedback is about encouragement, support and challenge from those you trust who are consistent in their support of you.

Recognizing and using defining moments well

I suggest that six attributes help us recognize and use defining moments well. These are: *see, seize, seek, stretch, still* and *soften* the moment.

See the moment

This is bringing objectivity and clarity and all our intellectual, emotional, physical and spiritual awareness. It is observing what is going on around us and understanding the dynamics and the interchange. It is allowing our emotional reactions to provide us with data, without those reactions distorting our decisions. Seeing is also about the capacity to watch and not rush into every situation. It is about getting the timing right and knowing when interventions are going to be most influential.

Seize the moment

This is being willing to grip the moment when action is needed and to say words of encouragement or directness when they are needed. It is being willing to take the first step. It is persuading others that now is the right time for action. It is not getting issues out of proportion but recognizing when action is necessary.

Seek the moment

This is more than watching. It might be following up an issue or practical concern and seeking an opportunity to make a difference. It might be seeking to support a particular cause. It will involve moving positively into a space where you can persuade and influence. It is taking the initiative and championing others.

Stretch the moment

This is not rushing on from one moment to another. It can be elongating a good moment; it can be stretching your thinking and doing the hard work of getting to the bottom of problems and then moving on.

Still the moment

This is creating shafts of stillness and providing moments for you and others when there can be reflection. It is stilling the moment so that there can be a new freshness and energy. It is believing strongly that stilling the moment is not a waste of time but is essential for long-term success.

Soften the moment

This is recognizing the impact that events have on others. It is thinking through their likely reaction so that difficult messages can be given in a way which enhances and does not diminish others. It is not about diluting a message, but it might be about softening the blow so that a message is understood and reacted to positively rather than destructively.

And where now?

May I leave you with the idea of defining moments as critical to your life? Some of your defining moments might be dramatic. At other times they might be the quiet realization that you are now in a different place with a different approach. As you celebrate your defining moments, may the memory of them enrich you. As you look forward, creating defining moments for those for whom you care can be a special gift. Do enjoy the rich variety of defining moments you have had, are now having and will have in the years ahead.

Selected bibliography

Adair, J. (2005), *How to Grow Leaders: The Seven Key Principles of Effective Leadership Development*, London: Kogan Page.

Allan, D., Kingdom, M., Murrin, K. and Rudkin, D. (1999), *?What If!: How to Start a Creative Revolution at Work*, Chichester: Capstone.

Archer, David and Cameron, Alex (2009), *Collaborative Leadership: How to Succeed in an Interconnected World*, Oxford: Elsevier.

Bibb, Sally and Kourdi, Jeremy (2004), *Trust Matters: For Organisational and Personal Success*, Basingstoke, UK: Palgrave Macmillan.

Boyatzis, Richard and McKee, Annie (2005), *Resonant Leadership*, Harvard, MA: Harvard Business School Press.

Buckingham, Marcus and Clifton, Donald O. (2004), *Now, Discover Your Strengths*, London: Pocket Books.

Buford, Bob (2001), *Stuck in Halftime*, Grand Rapids, MI: Zondervan.

Caplin, James (2008), *I Hate Presentations: Transform the Way You Present with a Fresh and Powerful Approach*, Chichester, UK: Capstone.

Charan, Ram (2009), *Leadership in the Era of Economic Uncertainty: The New Rules for Getting the Right Things Done in Difficult Times*, New York: McGraw-Hill.

Coffey, E. (2003), *10 Things That Keep CEOs Awake*, London: McGraw-Hill.

Collins, J. (2001), *Good to Great: Why Some Companies Make the Leap...and Others Don't*, New York: Harper Business.

Cottrell, Stephen (2007), *Do Nothing to Change Your Life: Discovering What Happens When You Stop*, London: Church House Publishing.

Covey, S. R. (1989), *The Seven Habits of Highly Effective People*, London: Simon & Schuster.

Dawson, Heather (2007), *Thriving in a Faster Faster World*, London: Praesta.

Hammond, John S., Keeney, Ralph L. and Raiffa, Howard (1999), "The Hidden Traps in Decision Making," *Harvard Business Review*, 76(5): 47–58.

Handy, C. (1997), *The Hungry Spirit*, London: Arrow.

Ind, Nicholas and Watt, Cameron (2004), *Inspiration: Capturing the Creative Potential of Your Organisation*, Basingstoke, UK: Palgrave Macmillan.

Kline, Nancy (1999), *Time to Think: Listening to Ignite the Human Mind*, London: Cassell Illustrated.

Leighton, Allan (2007), *On Leadership: Practical Wisdom from the People Who Know*, London: Random House Business Books.

Lencioni, Patrick (2002), *The Five Dysfunctions of a Team: A Leadership Fable*, San Francisco: Jossey-Bass.

O'Kelly, Eugene (2006), *Chasing Daylight: How My Forthcoming Death Transformed My Life*, New York: McGraw-Hill.

Radcliffe, Steve (2008), *Future, Engage, Deliver: The Essential Guide to Your Leadership*, Leicester, UK: Matador.

Shaw, Peter (2005), *Conversation Matters: How to Engage Effectively with One Another*, London: Continuum.

Shaw, Peter (2006), *Finding Your Future: The Second Time Around*, London: Darton, Longman and Todd.

Shaw, Peter (2006), *The Four Vs of Leadership: Vision, Values, Value-added and Vitality*, Chichester, UK: Capstone.

Shaw, Peter (2008), *Making Difficult Decisions: How to Be Decisive and Get the Business Done*, Chichester, UK: Capstone.

Shaw, Peter and Linnecar, Robin (2007), *Business Coaching: Achieving Practical Results through Effective Engagement*, Chichester, UK: Capstone.

Shaw, Peter and Stephens, Jane (2008), *Riding the Rapids: How to Navigate through Turbulent Times*, London: Praesta.

Stone, Beverley (2004), *The Inner Warrior: Developing Courage for Personal and Organisational Change*, Basingstoke, UK: Palgrave Macmillan.

Index